MW00899732

RESPECT: IT'S NOT ENOUGH!

ARTHUR H. MOONEYHAN

WESTBOW
PRESS®
A DIVISION OF THOMAS NELSON
& ZONDERVAN

This book is a work of non-fiction. Unless otherwise noted, the author and the publisher
make no explicit guarantees as to the accuracy of the information contained in this book
and in some cases, names of people and places have been altered to protect their privacy.

WestBow Press books may be ordered through booksellers or by contacting:

WestBow Press
A Division of Thomas Nelson & Zondervan
1663 Liberty Drive
Bloomington, IN 47403
www.westbowpress.com
1 (866) 928-1240

Because of the dynamic nature of the Internet, any web addresses or links contained in
this book may have changed since publication and may no longer be valid. The views
expressed in this work are solely those of the author and do not necessarily reflect the
views of the publisher, and the publisher hereby disclaims any responsibility for them.

Any people depicted in stock imagery provided by Getty Images are models,
and such images are being used for illustrative purposes only.
Certain stock imagery © Getty Images.

THE HOLY BIBLE, NEW INTERNATIONAL VERSION®, NIV® Copyright © 1973,
1978, 1984, 2011 by Biblica, Inc.® Used by permission. All rights reserved worldwide.

The Living Bible copyright © 1971 by Tyndale House Foundation. Used
by permission of Tyndale House Publishers Inc., Carol Stream, Illinois
60188. All rights reserved. The Living Bible, TLB, and the The Living
Bible logo are registered trademarks of Tyndale House Publishers.

Tree of Life (TLV) Translation of the Bible. Copyright © 2015
by The Messianic Jewish Family Bible Society.

ISBN: 978-1-9736-9086-3 (sc)
ISBN: 978-1-9736-9085-6 (hc)
ISBN: 978-1-9736-9087-0 (e)

Library of Congress Control Number: 2020909189

Print information available on the last page.

WestBow Press rev. date: 07/09/2020

CONTENTS

PART 1
WHERE IT ALL STARTS

PART 2
POSITIVE CHANGE IS ON THE HORIZON

PART 3
YOUR CHANGED HEART CHANGES EVERYTHING

FOREWORD

For those brave and courageous men and women who have already retired their badges of honor or continue to put on their uniforms with pride, working ludicrous hours because evil and crime never sleep. For you who are not there to hold your spouse or tuck in and comfort your precious children in the middle of the night because you are busy preserving and protecting our neighborhoods, properties, and freedoms. You who miss out on so many grand occasions, birthdays, holiday celebrations, personal family time, and so much more due to excessive mandatory hours and emergencies. When duty calls, you answer that call; your integrity will not let you do otherwise. You have put your life on hold and neglected that which is most important to you, through no fault of your own, but for the sake of your duty serving others. Those of you who make an immense sacrifice every day and night, leaving everything and everyone near and dear to you behind so you can protect and safeguard what is near and dear to us. Because heroes don't wear capes, they wear badges.

For those custody personnel who risk your lives walking through those doors and grill gates, into that treacherous facility of concrete and steel. You conduct those potentially dangerous escorts, respond to emergencies, and supervise the frequently unruly and often out-of-control inmate population.

You patrol our streets, highways, and byways responding to emergencies, continually having to return and combat your never-ending array of paperwork, documenting your involvement in your stress-inundated position. You sweat, bleed, and even cry for people you don't even know.

You answer the call to travel hundreds if not thousands of miles to protect our freedom, sacrificing everything because of the magnitude of your noble character, and your honor and dignity are such an intrinsic part of who you are. You perform the highest obligation and privilege of citizenship, bearing arms for your country.

Regardless of our insolence, you know there are good people of all races, creeds, and colors who need and request your protection and service. Your pride and integrity drive you ever forward. Dedication and loyalty are not just words to you—they are your lifestyle.

Please forgive us when we foolishly step out of line, open our mouths when we shouldn't, or fail to treat you with the utmost respect that you deserve, regardless of your ethnicity or gender.

Forgive us when out of our ignorance of not knowing the overall situation or circumstances, we exploit the foolish behavior of a wayward comrade while hundreds and thousands of you dedicated professionals remain steadfast in your duties every day.

Forgive us when we think that you should not react to our absurdity, while we disrespect you with our verbal tirade of threats and use of foul language, insulting your God-given authority and intelligence.

Please forgive us for all these things, "for we know not what we do." Thank you for your dedicated service, protection, and the extraordinary sacrifices that you make for us every day.

May our great God and Savior truly bless your hearts, careers, and families. Thank God for your loyalty to humanity.

INTRODUCTION

Before we start dissecting the topic of respect, I would like to begin by being a bit transparent about myself as well as the passion that fueled me to write this book. My father passed away when I was eleven years old. My father was by no means an ideal parent, husband, or role model, but at that stage in my young life, he was my strength and only example of dealing with life.

My father's passing left me in my home with my two older sisters and my mentally broken, unstable mother. After my dad's passing, my mom would frequently wake up abruptly after having horrible nightmares. She would wake up hysterical with grief, crying out in the middle of the night. These vivid and frightening dreams were about my dad calling her down into his grave. She would scream my name as loudly as she could, terrified, her heart pounding, wet with sweat and clammy hands. My mom soon attempted to pacify her condition with alcohol and numerous drugs to soothe her grief, which led to her being committed to a mental hospital. Our dysfunctional family broke up.

My two sisters went to live with an aunt and uncle who already had issues and problems with kids of their own. I went to live with my aunt and uncle in the Bay Area of California; they faced a similar situation with their family as well. My aunt and uncle took me into their home but made it very clear that I would never become a genuine part of their family.

Our dysfunctional family eventually got back together upon my mom's release from the mental hospital. We soon discovered that my mom's drinking issues had now turned into an alcohol and prescription medication addiction to appease her troubled life.

I was eleven years old when my life deteriorated. I cannot explain in words the overwhelming insecurities that I grew up with because I had to become the "man of the house" at eleven. Growing up, I felt robbed of my childhood, so I grew up depressed and angry at everything and everybody.

All over our planet, people from all different lifestyles are vying for any form of admiration or assurance of esteem that will bring them a sense of value, whether at home, on the job, at school, or anywhere we tread.

My background includes thirty years of working in the prison system in a custody position, with twenty-five of those years as a correctional sergeant. I am also an ordained Christian pastor and have served in numerous areas of the church through the years, both locally and internationally. I wasn't a Christian when I started working in the prison system, nor did I have any Christian upbringing. During my time in the prison system, I witnessed some of the most brutal, violent, and disgusting acts committed against humanity.

In this book, you will read true-life stories from the streets and inside the prison system. Unless otherwise noted, all the stories and examples in this book are my personal life experiences that I was directly involved in—not hearsay, but my own experiences. I have taken the liberty of changing names and rewording some verbal statements to protect personal identities and leave out the unnecessary exchange of foul and indecent language.

Through the years, I have observed a detrimental trend in our society and the world abroad. We have embraced the notion that being disrespectful toward each other and those in authority is acceptable. Almost everything in society is new and improved, including technology, living, industry, and communication. Changes to our everyday life cause alteration of human behavior. The primary purpose of the improvements is to make living easier and more comfortable. With all these gadgets and devices, video games, music, and social media, many people have become ungrateful and inconsiderate of the work accomplished in the past and the present. But it seems the most prominent degradation of current society is the insolence among relationships and lack of respect.

In this book, we will look at the relationships in our lives that cultivate, nurture, and help us develop lives of respect. We will take an in-depth look inside ourselves to discover why true feelings of trust, safety, and well-being are so important and where they derive.

You will view the inner structure of the prison system and the inmate population, along with the mental health program that governs inmate behavior. We will examine the causes, effects, and means to help cope with PTSD, often associated with careers in stress-filled occupations of criminal justice, military, and first responders. We will empathize and gain a newfound respect for these courageous men and women who serve and protect our streets, neighborhoods, highways, byways, and the world abroad, preserving and protecting our freedom. Take an epic wellness expedition on "your road through Samaria." Samaria will demand that you purge your very soul to find your individuality and figure out what is most important to you. This book will help you discover man's greatest objective in life, who the God of the Bible is, and how a relationship with Him can eradicate a life of shame and regret.

RESPECT: It's Not Enough! It is not just another book to read. You will be taking a journey. You will laugh, maybe even cry, but you will be changed! You will take a journey that so many of us need to experience to contend and cope with life, to end our search for significance in a mixed-up world, and examine our need for respect for each other and ultimately our Creator Himself.

OUR NEED FOR RESPECT

Respect: *a feeling or attitude of admiration and deference toward somebody or something, to show consideration or thoughtfulness in relation to and pay due attention and refrain from violating something or someone, a feeling of high regard, honor, or esteem.*

- Respect the law
- Respect another's privacy

Criminal justice personnel, military, and first responders have a much more difficult time conducting their jobs effectively without mutual respect. Nor can they give any sound instruction or enforce rules or the law appropriately. Respect is a mandatory element for the job position and is necessary to portray a positive image to the public and the inmates they supervise.

But respect or lack of respect goes so much further. It affects every single person in society. It becomes a vital essence of who we are or have become.

All human beings, at multiple points in their lives, strive for the fulfillment of being respected. Many will go to great lengths to gain and feel respected. But why do we have this overwhelming ambition *to be respected*? It has been said that gaining respect means that you are making a difference; people hold a high opinion of you. Everyone needs a sense of identity, and a fundamental way we get this is when others acknowledge and treat us as if we are important, and have a good reason to be here. There is an internal/external element to this need. Some need regular acknowledgment from other people, while those who possess sufficient self-respect are more internally driven. Not being taken seriously reduces our social status and hence our identities. When we are trivialized or ignored, we feel smaller and somehow less. As a result, we may become depressed, frustrated, or angry, and we may take revenge in subtle or public ways.

In many ways, respect defines who you are, how you are perceived, and how you are addressed and remembered. I'm sure that we could answer this above statement with an array of completely different personal responses, depending on what we have been exposed to and where we are at in this life journey. However, I have found some that I feel are quite intriguing; here are a few examples from BrainyQuote.

I'm not concerned with your liking or disliking me; all I ask is that you respect me as a human being.
—Jackie Robinson

Be peaceful, be courteous, obey the law, respect everyone; but if someone puts his hand on you, send him to the cemetery.
—Malcolm X

Respect your efforts, respect yourself. Self-respect leads to self-discipline. When you have both firmly under your belt, that's real power.
—Clint Eastwood

This world of ours must avoid becoming a community of dreadful fear and hate, and be instead, a proud confederation of mutual trust and respect.
—Dwight D. Eisenhower

That you may retain your self-respect, it is better to displease the people by doing what you know is right, than to temporarily please them by doing what you know is wrong.
—William J. H. Boetcker

It is so important to get respect for what you do and, at the same time, give it.
—Estelle Parsons

I firmly believe that respect is a lot more important, and a lot greater than popularity.

—Julius Erving

The bond that links your true family is not one of blood, but of respect and joy in each other's life.

—Richard Bach

Without feelings of respect, what is there to distinguish men from beasts?

—Confucius

As you can see from the examples, there is a vast difference in how we gain and think about respect. Think about it for just a moment. How do you know when you have earned the respect of others? During the span of your life, what lengths have you had to compromise or concede to feed your self-worth? Most of us have heard fancy statements such as "If you give respect, you will get it," or "Respect has to be earned." How about respect means you're making a difference, and people hold a high opinion of you? However, in my life, I have witnessed countless people who have spent the entirety of their lives attempting to earn or gain another's respect, only to realize that their best just wasn't good enough!

In the examples that we read, we can tend to overemphasize the contents of other's statements or life examples regarding respect. We attempt to apply their self-imposed "truth" in our own lives, only to find out that it might have worked for them but not for us. In many cases, respect seems to be the hardest thing to gain and the easiest thing to lose.

We are quick to manipulate or use people's lack of self-respect to our advantage to gain what we want, never considering the potential lifelong damage that we impose on others. We meander through life, holding our heads high while attempting to tread others under our feet. Therefore, our search for significance and respect goes on and on in an endless cycle, with no apparent end in sight.

In an article at Reference.com, this question is asked and answered:

Why is respect so important?

Quick Answer
Respect is important because it shows that one values another as an individual and that he honors the personal rights and dignity of the person as a fellow human being. People who are disrespectful often have few friends and alliances, and others do not enjoy being near them. Making good friends and warding off enemies is simpler when a person shows respect for others.

Full Answer
Respect goes a long way in developing a harmonious home, work, and social environment. Communication is clear and appropriate among individuals who respect each other. If a person is respectful, it shows that he has a positive attitude. A person who is courteous, listens to others, and treats people fairly is respectful. People who show respect for others often gain respect in return.

Respect is needed in the modern world to foster peace and kindness between all people. Partners who respect each other in relationships are much happier than those who do not. A child who respects the requests of his parents shows good character and obedience. Elderly people in nearly every culture command respect. In the business world, business leaders that show respect are more likely to form better partnerships and honor the requests of stakeholders. When managers and employees respect one another, they are able to communicate well and collaborate to reach business goals.

So just where does this journey end? Where can we find the source that will give us the self-assurance and confidence that we need to end our endless search for authentic lifelong and eternal significance?

Many people and stimuli influence our lives: parents, siblings, teachers, coaches, and spiritual leaders, along with our socioeconomic status. Let us start our journey and take a look at the most crucial relational and social contacts that establish and support the foundation of respect in our lives.

PART 1

WHERE IT ALL STARTS

CHAPTER 1

LEARN FROM AND GIVE RESPECT TO YOUR PARENTS

From our very inception, our most significant and the greatest influence to give and receive love and respect comes from our parents. Far from any other stimulus, our parents hold the top seed in shaping and molding who we are and who we eventually become.

It reminds me of the movie *Jumanji*, the part where Alan Parrish (played by Robin Williams) is speaking to the boy Peter (played by Bradley Pierce) right after the boy cheated in the Jumanji game and grew a tail and hair all over him. Alan is attempting to encourage the boy but catches himself verbally lashing out at the boy much the way his father had done to him. Alan stops himself and states, "Twenty-six years buried in the deepest darkest jungle, and I still turned out to be my dad." Many of us have spent numerous years in this jungle we call life, and whether we like it or not, we have been significantly shaped and molded by our parents.

It is a common phenomenon that a man will marry a woman who resembles his mother, just as a woman will marry a man who resembles her father. This spectacle commonly occurs even if the parent in question was an alcoholic or drug addict, verbally or physically abusive, neglectful, or, in a hundred different ways, a terrible example.

I remember working in the visiting room and entrance gate positions at the prison. It always amazed me why some of the women would visit regularly and then eventually marry the inmate confined inside the prison walls—and many times, an inmate serving a life sentence! I would think, *Aren't there any single men available outside on the street?*

One day I got into a conversation with an inmate's wife who was on her way to visit her husband inside the prison facility. When the question was brought up as to why she would marry an incarcerated man, she responded, "I was previously married to a man who was a physically, abusive alcoholic who ran around and cheated, just like my father. So, I married my current husband here in prison because the one thing that I know for sure is where he's at all night."

I am not the type of person who is often left speechless, but this was one of those moments! I was fortunate that she was in the process of walking by the entrance gate counter and soon out the door toward the visiting building when she made that statement, for I didn't have any idea what to say.

An overbearing mother can have quite a negative impact on her child. The official definition of overbearing: haughty, domineering, rudely arrogant, and very critical. The reason I now use the example of an overbearing mother is the simple fact that there are so many single mothers out there trying to raise their children, which I believe to be one of the most challenging jobs on the planet. You see, a single mother operates the difficult position of trying to be that loving, caring mother and yet taking on the day-to-day duties solo. Those duties, such as coping with sleeplessness, finding childcare, and paying bills, are no different than they are for a married mom. But you're on your own. In many instances, a single mother must become overbearing to deal with life, stress, and everyday responsibilities. Single mothers attempting to do their best in society and with their children should be held in high esteem since they have a most difficult task to do, often all alone or with little help.

There is no substitute for a husband and father who truly loves and respects his wife and then models that passion for his children, especially his precious daughter. In our society, we have an abundant number of women who fall victim to empty romances and painful relationships. These toxic relationships usually develop due to the void of their father's example of how a woman is to be cherished, loved, and respected in a deep and meaningful relationship. Our sweet little ladies are looking for true love and mutual respect in all the wrong places with all the wrong people, just hoping that the next one will bring true fulfillment.

I have two beautiful daughters. I remember neglecting my daughters of a father's love and adoration, especially my oldest daughter. Years went by as I remained so caught up in my job, church, sports, and just life in general. I didn't even realize the damage that my self-interest and neglect had been causing in our relationship.

One evening, I rushed to the hospital to see my eldest daughter, who was injured after she had wrecked our car. She was in a lot of pain, but the medical staff needed to assess her injuries. They were trying to roll her from side to side for examination as I was sitting on the bed next to her. She was moaning in intense pain as the medical staff shifted her body position. She looked me right in the eyes, and as if pleading for rescue, she called me "Daddy." That word sent a shock wave through my soul! She hadn't called me daddy since she was a little girl.

I immediately stood up and told the medical staff, "That's enough." The medical staff could easily discern by my tone of voice that I meant business. They gathered their equipment and left the room in a hurry. I had to apologize later, but they were hurting my girl; Daddy had to come to the rescue!

A short time later, while still in the hospital room, my wife and daughter were so engrossed in conversation that I just had to leave the room and take a walk. Initially, all I could think about was the immense honor and privilege bestowed on me to be my baby girl's "Daddy." Afterward, with my heart hurt and tears rolling down my cheeks, I reflected on my negligence, which caused me to take an in-depth look inside and rearrange my priorities.

Dads, they grow up so fast. We only have one go at raising our sweet little girls and being a positive example for our precious daughters.

I could go on and on using different examples of parental deficiency and the adverse results that affect us so greatly. However, I'm sure by this point you could use your life as an example and formulate your own personal scenarios. But the point is that we gain the lion's share of our identity from the roles that our parents have played in our lives, being good, bad, absent, or indifferent. As parents, it is nothing more than amazing how many ways we can find to mess up our own lives and then pass that negative inheritance down to our children.

It seems so unfair that we strive during the most significant part of our lives to measure up to and earn the respect of our parents, just to find out that our parents never found answers for or worked through their own issues. Caught in their maze of denial, shame, and regret, they have nothing to give. They are powerless to empower us with the love and respect that we need to contend with life. So, they pass on their pitiful shortcomings to us—the next generation.

CONTENDING WITH OUR PITIFUL WAYS

We can spend countless hours in therapy, receiving counsel about how it's not our fault or constructive coping tactics to survive the onslaught of destructive issues passed down from our parents that so harshly affect us. But is the problem gone? Or is it just covered up and disguised in another form of bad behavior or destructive emotions?

As I mentioned earlier, during my career, I worked at the entrance gate at the institutional facility. On Wednesday nights, AA (Alcoholics Anonymous) and NA (Narcotics Anonymous) groups would arrive at the institution to hold their weekly meetings with the inmate population. The outside sponsors would show up to the entrance facility and have to wait to be processed and escorted to their meeting location. I could easily tell who they were just by looking at them. For most of them, let's say their past seemed to be written all over their faces. And it was obvious where the group was hanging out because the cigarette smoke was so thick around them that it was hard to make out their faces through the cloud.

I thought, *So maybe they don't drink and take illegal drugs anymore. Fantastic!* But were their issues gone or just veiled? I engaged in conversation with many of the sponsors through the years, as well as many participants in the program in the institution and on the street. My assessment of their previous issues being gone, with most I would have to say absolutely not! I give them all credit for their commitment to rid their lives of these damaging and detrimental behaviors, and it's not my intention to degrade Alcoholics or Narcotics Anonymous in any way. I know for a fact that these important programs have helped millions of people overcome drug and alcohol addiction through the years. I only choose these two because I am a bit familiar with them. My point is simply this: Does AA, NA, or any other of the many rehab programs offer complete and total deliverance of the whole person in and of themselves, apart from a personal relationship with God? Or are our issues still a masquerade? Are we just placing a bandage on a gaping wound?

I want to make it clear that I am not trying to make you "religious." I know that many have misused that word, and others consider it taboo in their lives, and in many ways, I agree with you. But understand that in reality, we are all "religious." Whether you consider yourself agnostic, atheist, or any other category, I believe you still fall under the definition of being "religious." A partial definition would read as follows: Having or showing belief in and reverence for God or a deity, a god, goddess, or other being regarded as divine, somebody or something that is treated like a god. Whether we divinely regard or worship God, money, man, possessions, or a host of other things, we are all religious. That act of "belief and reverence" is just a matter of what is most important to you. Therefore, I am hoping we together can get over the "religious" word hang-up and stigma and put it behind us if one exists.

I have heard people make the most absurd comments as to whom or what God is—from an evil tyrant or sadist to a soft genie to be taken advantage of. My conclusion: all people know of a "god," whoever or whatever that god may be to them, but they know very little about the God of the Bible.

Therefore, my intention is to point out what the Bible would say to us. In the end, the decision is between you and God. I will attempt to pass on the same message that I heard and chose to receive, which has substantially impacted my life. No matter what you've done, who you've hurt, or bad choices you have made, you don't have to choose to live your life as a constant victim. You are not bound to being a product of your heritage, whether parental or any other influence of your present or past.

Please don't take my word for it. You will see it pointed out in the "From the Pastor's Side" section at the end of every chapter. However, I assure you everyone has a story to tell, and no two stories are the same, and you are the only one who can tell yours accurately. There are countless amounts of hurting, wounded, and lowly people suffering from the same or similar ills that you have suffered, and they need to hear your story, as they are looking for real answers. Yes, your story of temporal defeat, but more importantly, where you found the victory to conquer, overcome, and adapt in our crazy and mixed-up world.

The Scripture references that I will refer to in the "From the Pastor's Side" section at the end of each chapter are relatively simple and straightforward. However, Scripture in the Bible has been misinterpreted, manipulated, and misused for centuries. I have no intention of passing on that legacy in this book as I point out what the Bible would have to say to us. So, we need to apply a couple of simple ground rules to help us keep our Scripture references in the proper context.

1. Find a Bible and read at least five verses before and five verses after the given Scripture text to get the gist of the entire context.
2. Answer as many of the five *W*'s of Scripture interpretation as you can within the Scripture text itself: Who, What, Where, When, and Why.
    - *Who* is writing that particular segment of Scripture? To whom are they writing?
    - *What* is the subject matter that the writer is addressing at that moment and in that context?
    - *Where* is the writer's intended reader's location? What is their historical and cultural setting?
    - *When* in other parts of Scripture, is this statement, concept, or principle supported?
    - *Why* is this Scripture said or mentioned? Why at that time and to this person/people?

Let me give you just one example of the many ways that Scripture can easily be taken out of context or misinterpreted. There are two New Testament books directed to the Corinthians, consisting of First and Second Corinthians. In First Corinthians, the Apostle Paul writes the Christians in Corinth because they were struggling with their environment—surrounded by corruption and every conceivable sinful situation, they felt the pressure to adapt. The church was being undermined by immorality and spiritual immaturity. Paul heard of their issues and wrote the letter to address their problems and answer their questions. Paul confronts them about their sinful compromise and their need for corrective action, in a very direct manner.

In Second Corinthians, the Apostle Paul writes after the Corinthian believers had made some very positive changes in their behavior and conduct. The Apostle Paul's heart is unveiled like nowhere else in his New Testament writings. Paul writes with warm affection to celebrate his joy and renewed confidence in the Corinthians for their transformation and restored relationships.

First Corinthians is written primarily in a negative and direct context for correction. Second Corinthians was written after that positive change had occurred. If you utilize certain Scripture from First Corinthians in a positive manner, just as much as using Scripture from Second Corinthians with a negative approach, you will convey the wrong idea and impression of the writer and have therefore misinterpreted, manipulated, or misused the Scripture contents. This is just one example of the many ways to misrepresent Bible Scripture in its proper context.

By the way, in the "From the Pastor's Side" sections, you will often notice sentences in italic font. Those words in italic font are mine, me sharing my thoughts, statements, and so forth.

SCRIPTURE REFERENCES

Unless otherwise noted, all Scriptures are taken from the Holy Bible, New International Version (NIV). Copyright © 1973, 1978, 1984, 2011 by Biblica, Inc. Used by permission of Zondervan. Scripture references are also taken from The Living Bible (TLB).

The Lord speaks to Jeremiah just as He would to you or me. Jeremiah is just a man, and although we are not all prophets, you are not a mistake.

> Before I formed you in the womb, I knew you
> before you were born I set you apart;
> I appointed you as a prophet to the nations.
> (Jeremiah 1:5)

You are not forsaken.

> Though my father and mother forsake me,
> the Lord will receive me. (Psalm 27:10)

> Those who know your name trust in you,
> for you, LORD, have never forsaken those who seek
> you. (Psalm 9:10)

> Never! Can a mother forget her little child and not
> have love for her own son? Yet even if that should be,
> I will not forget you. (Isaiah 49:15) (TLB)

> He is a father to the fatherless; he gives justice to the
> widows, for he is holy. (Psalm 68:5) (TLB)

My youngest daughter was adopted at birth. She was about three years old, and we had just read the book of Ephesians when she stated to me with her beautiful and piercing big eyes, "Daddy, I'm really special. You were adopted once, but I was adopted twice!" Kids say the most inspiring things!

> For he chose us in him before the creation of the
> world to be holy and blameless in his sight. In love,
> he predestined us for adoption to sonship through

Jesus Christ, in accordance with his pleasure and will. (Ephesians 1:4–5)

Those in Christ receive no condemnation from God.

Therefore, there is now no condemnation for those who are in Christ Jesus, because through Christ Jesus, the law of the Spirit who gives life has set you free from the law of sin and death. (Romans 8:1–2)

No matter how good, bad, or indifferent your parents were, God offers us a new family.

All honor to God, the God and Father of our Lord Jesus Christ, for it is his boundless mercy that has given us the privilege of being born again so that we are now members of God's own family. Now we live in the hope of eternal life because Christ rose again from the dead. And God has reserved for his children the priceless gift of eternal life; it is kept in heaven for you, pure and undefiled, beyond the reach of change and decay. (1 Peter 1:3–4)

PARABLE OF THE LOST SON

This parable, told by Jesus, exemplifies God's willingness to forgive the worst of those who have sinned against him and extend his grace and mercy.

Jesus continued: "There was a man who had two sons. The younger one said to his father, 'Father, give me my share of the estate.' So he divided his property between them.

"Not long after that, the younger son got together all he had, set off for a distant country and there squandered his wealth in wild living. After he had spent everything, there was a severe famine in that whole country, and he began to be in need. So he went and hired himself out to a citizen of that country, who sent him to his fields to feed pigs. He longed to fill his stomach with the pods that the pigs were eating, but no one gave him anything.

"When he came to his senses, he said, 'How many of my father's hired servants have food to spare, and here I am starving to death! I will set out and go back to my father and say to him: Father, I have sinned against heaven and against you. ¹⁹ I am no longer worthy to be called your son; make me like one of your hired servants.' So he got up and went to his father.

"But while he was still a long way off, his father saw him and was filled with compassion for him; he ran to his son, threw his arms around him and kissed him.

"The son said to him, 'Father, I have sinned against heaven and against you. I am no longer worthy to be called your son.'

"But the father said to his servants, 'Quick! Bring the best robe and put it on him. Put a ring on his finger and sandals on his feet. Bring the fattened calf and kill it. Let's have a feast and celebrate. For this son of mine was dead and is alive again; he was lost and is found.' So they began to celebrate.

"Meanwhile, the older son was in the field. When he came near the house, he heard music and dancing. So he called one of the servants and asked him what was going on. ²⁷ 'Your brother has come,' he replied, 'and your father has killed the fattened calf because he has him back safe and sound.'

"The older brother became angry and refused to go in. So his father went out and pleaded with him. But he answered his father, 'Look! All these years I've been slaving for you and never disobeyed your orders. Yet you never gave me even a young goat so I could celebrate with my friends. But when this son of yours who has squandered your property with prostitutes comes home, you kill the fattened calf for him!'

"'My son,' the father said, 'you are always with me, and everything I have is yours. But we had to celebrate and be glad, because this brother of yours was dead and is alive again; he was lost and is found.'
(Luke 15:11-32)

CHAPTER 2

FRIENDS, CUZ, DOGS, AND HOMIES

Just in case the title of this chapter doesn't spell it out clearly enough, we will be looking at how our friends and colleagues influence and affect us in fostering a life of respect.

I like to consider life in seasons: you are a baby and toddler for a season; you are a child and a kid for a season; a teenager, a young adult, and so on. If we could only skip to, say, season four for a year or so and then go back with that knowledge to help us through childhood and our teen years. That is, of course, if we would use this knowledge constructively during this formidable time of our lives. I think all of us have thought about the idea of going back to relive certain parts of our lives and do things differently.

My oldest daughter is now well into her young adult years. We still laugh at her actions when she was a teenager. She would hang out with her friends and come back home with the answers to all *life's questions, every question past, present, and future.* Those teenagers with very little to no life experience had figured it all out! So, I would look at her with a serious look on my face and tell her, "Tiffany, please! For God's sake and the sake of all humanity, please write your book now while you have all the answers, and know everything, because in a few years, when you figure out that your information is wrong, well, it will be devastating." She would usually look at me with a smirk on her face and say, "Very funny, Dad," and then walk away.

Quite a few years ago, I was a youth pastor; I was in the process of raising a teenage son and daughter of my own. Therefore, I got the privilege to see and experience the adolescent years firsthand, through the lives of the teenagers that I was already working within the youth ministry. One thing that I learned from that experience is the huge impact that friends can have on each other and their desperate need to fit in with their crowd. The lengths that a young person will go through to gain and retain respect from one's peers is nothing short of mind-boggling. Every week we would have games and activities to attempt to have the kids bond as a group, break down personal barriers, and hopefully meet some new friends. It was extremely rare when new relationships ensued due to our efforts, for normally right after the activities were over, the kids would hurriedly return to their previous group of friends without reservation. Teenagers do have to deal with stress and other emotional issues. But from my experience, one of the most powerful influences in a teenager's life is the need to belong and fit in—to be accepted by those they consider their peer group.

In prison, the pressure to find your comfort group is immense. A majority of the inmate population is separated either by their ethnicity, their gang affiliation, or both. These two factions are the chief contributors governing the conduct and freedom that inmates will have in most correctional facilities during their incarceration. Just being in the wrong place at the wrong time, or speaking with the wrong people, could cause major upheaval—or even possibly cost you your life. They call it "prison politics," and the political rules in prison are quite a bit different from those on the street.

I used to like to find creative ways to catch inmates off guard and help them think about some of the stupid choices they were making. In one of the prisons where I was working, certain gang factions declared that their fellow gang members could not do time at that particular facility. At one time, this institution was a "PC" (protective custody), or "rat joint." Some of the inmates housed there at one time had testified in court regarding the gang's destructive and violent activity or debriefed to terminate their membership with the gang they were associated with, which made them no good in the active gang members' eyes.

The active gang members were ordered not to serve time in the mainline at that facility. If they disobeyed, they would no longer remain in good status with the gang. So, when one of their gang members got transferred to this prison yard, he was to attack another inmate violently and get taken off the yard and put into "lockup" or administrative segregation and transferred to a different institution. After the inmate was transferred to a different institution, his fellow gang members would approach him and demand his institutional paperwork to ensure the gang's protocol had been followed according to the instructions. Along with that act of violence, the inmate would receive additional time in prison, and violence went on his record if violence on his record didn't already exist prior, along with other negative repercussions.

When I had the opportunity to speak with the inmate alone after his act of violence, and before he left the yard for the lockup unit, I would try to help him reflect on the foolish choice he just made. The conversation would go something like this:

"So, your old lady must not be very good-looking, huh?"

"What do you mean by that?"

"Well, you will do what homie says on the yard. Go out there, get in a fight with someone, and do more time. But you won't do right by your woman to go home in time to take care of her and your kids, so I'm thinking homie must be better-looking than your old lady, so obviously, she's not very pretty!

"Look, I just insulted you to get your attention. Do you think that homie cares about you or whether you ever see your family again? They are just using you. Look, I'm not trying to be your dad or preach to you; I'm just trying to help you think about these stupid choices you are making. Right now, if they thought you were 'telling,' giving up some information, or if you didn't do what they said to get off the yard, they would beat you down or bury a shank in your neck! That's how much they care about you."

"They do care about me. We have each other's back; we look out for each other!"

"The people who care about you are on the streets, crying and praying for you every night, those who tried to help you make positive life choices, to stay away from knuckleheads like your fellow gang members, and stay out of a place like this. Your wife, kids, mom, dad, grandparents, aunts and uncles, and family are the people who care about you! You remember your mom or some other family member telling you not to hang out with these guys, saying, 'They will only get you into trouble?' Well, look where you are. This whole time you should have been listening to those people who love and care about you and tried to help you do the right thing! Not these knuckleheads, who couldn't care less whether you ever get out of prison or see those family members on the street who truly love and care about you ever again!"

I had some amazing results, conversations, and feedback over the years. I even had a few occasions where the inmate in question would decide not to go to the segregation unit and make an immediate change regarding his gang status. Then choose to remain in the general population, attempt to behave and program, following the institutional rules and regulations. It's remarkable how different young men or women will respond when removed from their gang or group and you can verbally communicate candidly, without the pressure of the pack.

THE POWER OF THE PACK

This issue of respect among friends or colleagues is a powerful and often controlling concern. You see, it doesn't matter what label happens to be the title of your "pack." All of us strive to measure up and earn our acceptance and status in the pecking order. In the previous example, I referenced the pack as being that of a gang, but packs come in a variety of classifications: ethnic divisions, jocks, druggies, intellectuals, or any other gathering of individuals with whom you associate. They all represent different forms of packs that we so easily become caught up in an attempt to earn our status.

I remember having a conversation with my medical doctor a few years back. We had become friends over the years, and we would talk quite candidly with each other. He was a very intelligent and well-respected man in his medical field and the community. He had worked at the prison where I worked on a part-time basis for many years. He had seemingly become friends and developed friendships with quite a few of the correctional officers who would transport inmates in and out of the hospital/clinic to be interviewed and treated by him and other doctors in the hospital.

He went on to tell me that the minute that he stopped working at the prison hospital and would see these correctional officers at the hospital clinic downtown, that they would completely ignore him. "They just walk by pridefully, as if they had never seen me before, even refusing to make eye contact." He went on to talk about how almost all the correctional officers were stricken with pride and walked around with their chests out and arms back because they thought they were tough guys.

I explained to him that I wasn't about to defend the actions of our custody staff and that in many cases, what he described was probably true. However, I also mentioned to him that pride rears its ugly head in many forms and many ways. That statement seemed to catch him off guard, and he asked me, "What do you mean by that?" I went on to tell him that I presently work in a mental health quad, interacting with and surrounded by many highly educated psychiatrists and psychologists.

Many times, during our interactions, they'd talk down to me and other custody staff members as if we were inept, uneducated, and didn't have a brain in our heads! They tend to pridefully tilt their heads backward, pointing their noses upward, while rolling their eyes in seeming disgust because they are just so much better, smarter, and there is just no way to make us uneducated knuckle-dragging morons understand anything. He couldn't help himself—he just had to break out and laugh at that one! But being the great person that he is, and with the intellectual environment that so dominated his life, I think it gave him something to ponder.

Here is something to think about, a short lesson on wisdom and knowledge, from gotquestions.org.

> **Question:** "What is wisdom? What is the difference between wisdom and knowledge?"
>
> **Answer:** Wisdom and knowledge, both recurring themes in the Bible, are related but not synonymous. The dictionary defines *wisdom* as "the ability to discern or judge what is true, right, or lasting." *Knowledge*, on the other hand, is "information gained through experience, reasoning, or acquaintance." Knowledge can exist without wisdom, but not the other way around. One can be knowledgeable without being wise. Knowledge is knowing how to use a gun; wisdom is knowing when to use it and when to keep it holstered.
>
> Knowledge is what is gathered over time through the study of the Scriptures. It can be said that wisdom, in turn, acts properly upon that knowledge. Wisdom is the fitting application of knowledge. Knowledge understands the light has turned red; wisdom applies the brakes. Knowledge sees the quicksand; wisdom walks around it. Knowledge memorizes the Ten Commandments; wisdom obeys them. Knowledge learns of God; wisdom loves Him.

The point is that we are greatly impacted by the influence of our friends, family, colleagues, and peer groups. This influence can be positive, negative, or potentially harmful. These groups generally shape the beliefs and attitudes we hold regarding what opportunities are available to us, the direction our lives will go, and ultimately where our beliefs, reverence, and respect will resolve.

Teach us to number our days,
that we may gain a heart of wisdom. (Psalm 90:12)

For the LORD gives wisdom;
from his mouth come knowledge and understanding.
For wisdom will enter your heart,
and knowledge will be pleasant to your soul.
(Proverbs 2:6–10)

For the foolishness of God is wiser than human wisdom, and the weakness of God is stronger than human strength.
(1 Corinthians 1:25)

Growing old is mandatory; growing up is optional!

One who has unreliable friends soon comes to ruin,
but there is a friend who sticks closer than a brother.
(Proverbs 18:24)

Though I walk in the midst of trouble,
you preserve my life.
You stretch out your hand against the anger of my foes;
with your right hand you save me. (Psalm 138:7)

The following Scripture has always been special to me, but I need to set the stage just a bit. The prophet Samuel was instructed by God to go to the house of Jesse to anoint God's king after the people's king. King Saul was compelled to do things his way and disobeyed God, and God rejected him as king.

When Samuel arrived at the house of Jesse, Samuel was impressed with one of Jesse's sons in particular because he was a big man and a warrior in King Saul's army. God set the mission straight and said the following.

But the LORD said to Samuel, "Do not consider his appearance or his height, for I have rejected him. The LORD does not look at the things people look at. People look at the outward appearance, but the LORD looks at the heart." (1 Samuel 16:7)

CHAPTER 3

HOW WE RESPECT AND CATEGORIZE PEOPLE

Have you ever put much thought into how we all put people into categories? We tend to assume that how we view people warrants some credibility as to how we should approach or treat another person. If we have somehow had a bad experience with a certain ethnicity, for example, that's how we should deal with all these types of people!

In the prison system, racial imbalance and cultural disorientation are always infused with potential mayhem among the inmate population. I mentioned earlier about the pressure to fit in and find your comfort group. In many cases, it's a matter of survival, regardless of how you relate to people of opposing racial or cultural differences. I was involved with several incidents where racial or cultural issues reared their ugly heads in prison, causing major upheaval among the inmate population for different reasons.

In some cases, these diverse issues were due to racial or cultural misunderstandings. Here are a few of my personal life examples in and out of prison.

DISGRACEFUL RACIAL PREJUDICE

At one period during my tenure with the prison system, my assignment was a yard sergeant in one of the general population yards. The prison yard and outdoor facilities had to be constantly maintained; therefore, an inmate yard crew was assigned to handle this task of yard maintenance. The lead man on the inmate yard crew was a large black inmate. We will say his name was Perry. He stood about six feet five inches tall and had a steadfast reputation on the yard. He was serving a life sentence, and he was from the deep southern portion of the United States.

The other inmate yard crew workers respected Perry due to his work ethic and stature, as he spent a lot of time every day on the weight pile lifting heavy weights, and he was strong and well built. The other inmates assigned to the yard crew did their jobs and did what Perry told them to do. No other inmate in his right mind would want Perry angry and searching for him because he didn't complete his work assignment or neglected instructions!

Over time, Perry and I became well acquainted with each other, and we would talk on the yard about a host of different issues. Eventually, our conversations became quite personal as we developed a mutual respect. Inmate Perry explained to me the unfortunate tragedies that he was subjected to growing up in the Deep South: separate bathrooms for black people, black people sitting at the back of the bus, and so on. As he continued explaining, I felt completely distressed and terrible about the unthinkable prejudice that Perry had been subjected to when he was younger. Being from California my whole life, I had no idea that such horrendous acts had actually taken place—or maybe I was just in denial about the terrible ways that people can treat each other. Either way, I was disgraced, disgusted, and ashamed.

Perry had mentioned to me that he heard other inmates on the yard mention that I was a Christian, and he then stated that he was a Muslim. Our conversation started heading off in the direction of religion. At this point in our rapport, I felt quite comfortable being candid in our discussions. When I'd say something that Perry didn't like, he would throw his arms up over his head in disgust while mumbling his disapproval and walking away. He always came back, though—many times later that day, if not the following.

One day as our conversations progressed, I asked Perry, "What is your definition of love?"

He twisted his head side to side and back and forth as if either he was trying to think or maybe was just challenged by the question. He eventually answered, "Well, it's the way you feel … toward someone you care about."

I told him that his great answer would partially describe the byproduct of love, but not the definition. So, I challenged him to read what's referred to as the "love" chapter in the Bible, found in 1 Corinthians 13:1–13. He had already told me that he had an old King James Version of the Bible in his cell, which his grandmother had given him many years ago, and that was the only Bible that he trusted.

The next morning, I was standing in the middle of the yard when the buildings were unlocked, and the inmates were released. Perry came straight for me at a fast pace. He was smiling as I had never seen him smile before. He walked right up to me and said, "Sergeant, I have never … I couldn't stop. I would put it down and read it again; I was up all night." It was as if he was so excited and amazed that he couldn't complete his train of thought or finish a sentence. We talked a bit back and forth regarding his relationship with God and the definition of love. Then he quite abruptly stated, "This isn't about me changing up and coming to that blond-haired, blue-eyed surfer god Jesus, is it?"

I told him, "I don't know. Is it?"

Just then, Perry did what he did best: he threw his hands up over his head, mumbled something, and walked away. This time it took Perry a couple of days to come back to talk on the yard, but it gave me some time to think and pray. The next time Perry approached me, I had a few things that I felt I needed to say to him. Perry found me in the middle of the yard and drew near as if he wanted to converse. We spoke for a while, and I asked him where he got the impression that Jesus was a blond-haired, blue-eyed surfer dude, and I couldn't help but think that statement was funny.

As he stood there with a blank look on his face, I explained to him that my understanding of the Jewish culture during Jesus's time dictated that the higher, wealthier echelon had brighter, lighter skin. Jesus was from a very poor family, and therefore his skin was more than likely dark. How dark I don't know, but not the bright white skin tone that he was talking about. Perry seemed a bit taken back when I told him that I was sorry and completely perplexed over the shameful racism and discrimination that he lived through as a black man growing up in the South; that I couldn't imagine how degraded and disrespected he felt. But I told him that he was an easy read, and the reason that he wouldn't consider Jesus was his hatred for the white man and that if he didn't find a way to get over that, he would remain a victim of his past. It would eat him alive inside! Perry again followed his protocol and threw his arms up over his head, mumbling his disapproval and eventually stating, "We talk a lot … about a lot of different things, even personal issues, and I don't hate you." I said that I appreciated his recognition but that he and I both knew I was a rare exception.

THE CUBAN REVOLT—CULTURAL MISUNDERSTANDING?

A short time after I started with the prison system in the early 1980s, we had quite a large influx of Cuban inmates that assimilated into our correctional institutions after the Freedom Flotilla, whereby Cuba's President Fidel Castro allowed thousands to leave the country. Other Cuban citizens were exported forcibly from their home country as well. Many of these forced exports were criminals and mental patients. I have a feeling that we didn't screen the incursion of the incoming Cuban population very well, and President Castro took advantage of the situation and sent us a large populace of his "less-than-upstanding citizens."

We received a large group of Cuban criminals on the prison yard at California Correctional Institution, the facility where I was working at the time. We had very little intel (or intelligence) regarding anything about these inmates. Many of the Cuban inmates were covered with bizarre tattoos that were completely foreign to any of us as correctional employees, and they were not about to volunteer any information to make our jobs easier. You see, in the prison system, reading and identifying tattoos can tell you a great deal about individuals, such as what gang or group they are involved with and what rank they hold, what neighborhood they are from, and a whole lot more vital information. We had none of this information at our disposal. So virtually, we had a large group of potentially violent inmates that we knew little to nothing about, and very few spoke any English, so we were short on communication as well. The Cuban inmates walked the yard together; they sat together during feeding times, and they never seemed to want to be separated for any reason.

One early evening during the dinner feeding, one of our correctional officers had a verbal disagreement with one of the Cuban inmates in the dining room. The inmate continued to be uncooperative and verbally disrespectful, so the officer ordered him out of his seat, told him to place his hands against the dining room wall, and searched him for weapons and contraband. The officer then put him in handcuffs. As the officer was escorting the inmate out of the dining room and across the yard toward the watch office to quell the situation, we got a call from the nearest tower position on the radio, informing us to turn around because we had company.

We turned around to see that all the Cuban inmates present in the dining room were now standing outside, about fifty or so yards away, staring directly at us and not looking at all happy. Seconds later, they came running as fast as they could directly at us, and an all-out brawl with custody staff ensued. The brawl took place on the medium facility yard, so the only gun tower coverage that we had were perimeter towers that were quite a distance away from the incident. They were rendered helpless anyway due to the mix of staff and inmates combined in the immediate area. If any of the tower officers were to shoot in an attempt to quell the situation, more than likely, both staff and inmates would be injured or struck by the tower officer's discharge of the incoming projectile.

The brawl lasted fewer than three minutes or so, but when you are in the middle of it, it seems like a much longer duration of time! Afterward, we all felt a bit fortunate that either the Cubans didn't have enough time on the yard to acquire weapons or they didn't have them with them at the time. Although minor, there were plenty of staff injuries. But no weapons were reported as being used during the disturbance.

At this point in my career, we didn't have nonlethal weapons such as pepper spray and side-handle batons that we acquired to carry on our person years later, so a majority of our job consisted of physical interaction during a disturbance or hand-to-hand combat.

A couple of weeks after the incident occurred, I was assigned as an IE, an investigative employee. My job as an investigative employee was to interview one of the Cuban inmates involved in the altercation with staff and file a written report of my interview for the disciplinary process. As I was interviewing the inmate for my report, he told me something interesting that I would never forget. He stated that the staff members forced the Cuban inmates to fight and that they didn't have a choice! He went on to explain that when that officer handcuffed the Cuban inmate right in front of the other Cubans, it was extremely disrespectful. "It would be the same in your country if I walked up to you and spit directly into your face. That's how disrespectful it was. So, you made us take action and fight you!"

Now, there was no way that I felt the Cuban inmates were in any way justified in their physical attack on staff. However, it did give my coworkers and me a lot to think about regarding the potential cultural misconceptions that we could be facing in the future while interacting with the Cuban inmates and others from distant places.

AFRICA MISSION TRIP

In 2008, my youngest daughter and I, along with seventeen people from our local church, went on a mission trip to Rwanda, Africa. That's right, Rwanda, where the terrible genocide of 1994 claimed almost a million lives in approximately ninety days.

While at our home church in Gisenyi, I was speaking to one of the young men who was a teacher at the on-grounds educational facilities. During our conversation, he told me that he was Patrick's brother. Patrick was one of our van drivers who had been driving us around from place to place. Earlier that day, Patrick had mentioned to me that he was married and had a family. So, I said to his brother John, "Hey, John, just curious, but you are a handsome, intelligent young man. Your brother is married; why aren't you?" John explained to me that he would love to be married and have a family of his own, but that he couldn't afford a "cow." You see, in Rwanda, when a man asks for a woman's hand in marriage, he is to replace her presence in the home with a cow, which would benefit the family after she was gone. John also informed me that sometimes you could negotiate a cash settlement or other animals as well. But the cow was the accepted standard payment for your new bride being removed from her home to marry.

We had a young woman on the trip with us, and we will call her Polly. Polly was a lot of fun and was great with the kids, but she proved to be a bit clumsy. She was constantly breaking the freshly made bricks and cement blocks that we had made to construct latrines that we were building. A couple of the other guys and I started making fun of her. She would walk by, and we would say things to her like, "Hey, Polly, don't be walking too close to that building; you might knock it down." She would smile and usually return some sarcastic statement back at us, and we would all break out and laugh.

John was well aware of her being clumsy and how we were having a few laughs at her expense. As he was explaining to me in more detail about the payoff to buy a bride in Rwanda, she just happened to walk right in front of us. I said to him, "Hey, John, we both know Polly can't be worth a whole cow, so what would she be worth, a dead goat and a couple of chickens?" He broke out laughing and said we would have to negotiate that with her father!

We all approach life and other people with certain amounts of our agendas, regardless of where that stimuli or stigma generates. We approach people with our preconceived notions, prejudiced thoughts, and cultural hang-ups. Yes, we are all guilty! Our predetermined mindsets make it impossible to take each person as an individual, to treat everyone with equal respect and dignity, no matter where they are from, what they believe, or the color of their skin. It is very difficult for us to look beyond our predetermined conclusions, to engage all people in a deep and meaningful conversation where we both get beyond the masks we wear to cover up who we really are. This world would be a much better place if we could avoid wearing these phony make-believe masks to hide behind or deceive. So, I guess the question that we have to ask ourselves is, "Is it possible?"

For the eyes of the Lord are on the righteous
and his ears are attentive to their prayer,
but the face of the Lord is against those who do evil.
(1 Peter 3:12)

Years ago, my youngest daughter came home from school and mentioned that one of the kids was mean to her and that she didn't like this girl. I told her that was fine as long as she loved her. She looked at me as if I'd bumped my head! When I explained to her that liking someone is optional but loving them is not, it is not easy, but we are all a work in progress.

Above all, love each other deeply, because love covers over a multitude of sins. (1 Peter 4:8)

Your love, LORD, reaches to the heavens, your faithfulness to the skies. (Psalm 36:5)

Forgiving is never easy but is essential—or we seem to remain the victim.

Love is patient, love is kind. It does not envy, it does not boast, it is not proud. It does not dishonor others, it is not self-seeking, it is not easily angered, it keeps no record of wrongs. [6] Love does not delight in evil but rejoices with the truth. [7] It always protects, always trusts, always hopes, always perseveres. (1 Corinthians 13:4–7)

And when you stand praying, if you hold anything against anyone, forgive them, so that your Father in heaven may forgive you your sins. (Mark 11:25)

Whoever is kind to the poor lends to the LORD, and
he will reward them for what they have done.
(Proverbs 19:17)

For he has rescued us from the dominion of darkness
and brought us into the kingdom of the Son he loves,
in whom we have redemption, the forgiveness of sins.
(Colossians 1:13–14)

I will give you a new heart and put a new spirit in you;
I will remove from you your heart of stone and give
you a heart of flesh. (Ezekiel 36:26)

*Whether family/friend/enemy, jock, bookworm, and so forth, God puts
us in only one of two categories:*

- *Those He loves and have been made alive in Christ*
- *Those He loves and needs to be made alive in Christ*

PART 2

POSITIVE CHANGE
IS ON THE HORIZON

CHAPTER 4

OUR SOCIAL AND PSYCHOLOGICAL INTERVENTION

Many centuries before Sigmund Freud (1856–1939), a renowned psychologist, physiologist, and great thinker during the early twentieth century, who is referred to as the Father of Psychoanalysis, we have tried to identify a method for evaluating and treating mental illness and deriving a solid explanation for human behavior. Sigmund

Freud and many other well-meaning psychologists and sociologists throughout the centuries have evaluated, diagnosed, and attempted to treat or understand these conditions. Their primary vehicles for their research and development were psychology and sociology; therefore, let us look at a brief definition of these systems. (*Merriam-Webster* and verywellmind.com)

> Sociology: Scientific study of society, patterns of social relationships, social interaction, and study of human values, relationships, culture, and beliefs, inclusive of the systematic study of development, structure, and collective behavior of organized groups of human beings.

> Psychology: A broad field that encompasses the study of human thought, behavior, development, personality, emotion, motivation, and more. Gaining a richer and deeper understanding of psychology can help people achieve insights into their own actions, as well as a better understanding of others. Among the major goals of psychology are to describe, explain, predict, and improve human behavior to help people live better lives.

Sociology is the study of human social behavior, while psychology's focus is more on the individual human mind and conduct. Although there are several different branches of psychology in this chapter, we will be taking a closer look at the area of clinical psychology that is primarily concerned with the assessment and treatment of mental illness and psychiatric problems.

For those of us not familiar with the California Department of Corrections and Rehabilitation's (CDCR's) prison system's mental health function, the following information is a brief overview copied directly from the online (Mental Health Services Delivery System's (MHSDS) program guide.

The California Department of Corrections and Rehabilitation (CDCR) Mental Health Services Delivery System (MHSDS) provides inmates access to mental health services. The MHSDS is designed to provide an appropriate level of treatment and to promote individual functioning within the clinically least restrictive environment consistent with the safety and security needs of both the inmate-patient and the institution.

The intent of the MHSDS is to advance the CDCR's mission to protect the public by providing timely, cost-effective mental health services that optimize the level of individual functioning of seriously mentally disordered inmates and parolees in the least restrictive environment. The MHSDS has been functioning in CDCR since 1994. The MHSDS utilizes a variety of professional clinical, custody, and support staff to provide the best available quality of care to seriously mentally disordered inmates.

Any inmate can be referred for mental health services at any time. Inmates who are not identified at reception or upon arrival at an institution as needing mental health services may develop such needs later. Any staff members that have concerns about an inmate's mental stability are encouraged to refer that inmate for evaluation by a qualified mental health clinician (psychiatrist, psychologist, or clinical social worker). Under certain circumstances, referral to mental health may be mandatory. A referral to mental health should be made whenever any of the following occurs:

- An inmate demonstrates possible symptoms of mental illness or a worsening of symptoms. An inmate verbalizes thoughts of suicide or self-harm behavior.
- Upon return from court when an inmate has received bad news such as a new sentence that may extend their time.
- An inmate has been identified as a possible victim per the Prison Rape Elimination Act.
- An inmate demonstrates sexually inappropriate behavior per the exhibitionism policy.
- An inmate who is written up for a disciplinary infraction was demonstrating bizarre, unusual, or uncharacteristic behavior when committing the infraction.

- An inmate placed into administrative segregation indicates suicidal potential on the prescreening, or rates positive on the mental health screening, or gives staff any reason to be concerned about the inmate's mental stability, such as displaying excessive anxiety.
- Upon arrival to an institution when the inmate indicates prior mental health treatment and medications, especially if not previously documented.

Additional programs exist within the system; however, there are two primary classifications of inmates in CDCR's Mental Health Services and Delivery System's (MHSDS) program:

1. Correctional Clinical Case Management System, referred to as triple CMS
2. Enhanced Outpatient Program (EOP), EOP being the more severe of the two

For quite a few years during my tenure with the prison system, I worked with mentally ill inmates in all classifications and stages of mental illness. A majority of the mentally ill inmates depended heavily on the intervention of the mental health staff and their issued medication to function on an everyday basis, and we, as the correctional custody staff, were usually the first line of contact and intervention when a crisis occurred with the inmate population. Our crisis intervention as custody staff was a constant, ongoing job responsibility multiple times every day as we attempted to work in accord with our mental health-care staff.

Working with the inmates in this classification was an entirely different experience than working with inmates in the general population. The inmates in the MHSDS would operate to the beat of a different drum, quite often exhibiting bizarre, irrational, and even violent behavior, explaining that the "voices told them to do it." With a general population inmate, you could somewhat predict or at least anticipate an inmate's behavior, but with an inmate who was mentally ill, their behavior could change instantly without warning to violent, delusional, or hallucinatory. Fighting with or without weapons, staff assaults, and suicide by cutting or hanging were all common events, along with several incidents involving inappropriate sexual behavior, to mention a few.

Along with the issue of inmate behavior, we had an ongoing problem with the mental health and custody staff working together in harmony. Other than the typical personality conflicts, the mental health staff would tend to look at things from the viewpoint of the inmate being more of a patient, and custody staff tended to view the inmate population as inmates or convicted felons.

As a correctional program sergeant, I dealt with the chore of reviewing and processing the quad's inmate disciplinary paperwork. All of the MHSDS inmate disciplinary paperwork had to be sent to the mental health department to be evaluated to determine the inmate's involvement and state of mind and use of medication during the violation. The serious rule violations the mental health staff assigned to the inmate's caseload would have to be submitted as a written report, as part of the disciplinary due process paperwork package to assist custody staff in determining the punishment needed in the hope of correcting wrongful behavior.

Every mental health report that I remember receiving back from the mental health department read in a similar way. That the inmate is not responsible for his actions for different reasons; the primary reason was that the inmate didn't take his prescribed medication, or at least that's what he told his mental health practitioner. From a very obvious cynical viewpoint, many of our custody staff members would frown on this response and mention how the psych department was again making excuses for the inmate's poor behavior. As I would examine these reports, a couple of recurring thoughts would frequently pass through my mind: *How can an inmate in this condition ever gain a life of self-respect, being that they are so dependent on this medication? And what are the mental health staff's tools to harvest positive change in a mentally ill inmate's life?*

MENTAL HEALTH STAFF RESPONSE

I had numerous conversations with our mental health staff in prison regarding intervention, counseling, and treatment of the inmate's mental health conditions. The consensus from a majority, but not all, was that the three intricate parts of a human being are body, mind, and spirit. Let me give an example of how the three break down, according to an online resource called Kezominde.

- Body: Natural external world: smell, feel, taste, hear, sight. (*Physiological relates to the environment.*)
- Soul: Personality: mind, will, emotions. (Physiological relates to the intellectual realm.)
- Spirit: Intuition, conscience, communication. (*Spiritual relates to God*)

The mental health staff was well equipped to help with the body and partly with the soul but were entirely out of their element when it came to the spirit. Therefore, in essence, they were doing their best but applying a two-part solution to a three-part healing process. So just what happens when this third part is neglected or rejected? Prescribe medications—and lots of them—to numb or neutralize the spirit. Our pill dispensary lines in the mental health quad took longer than to feed the entire unit of the inmate population!

I remember when the institution started the MHSDS Mental Health Services Delivery System. All of us supervisors were required to attend an eight-hour class to help get us on board with and understand the program. Two on-staff psychiatrists taught the MHSDS class. A common statement that they would mention during the class was that there is "no cure for mental health." Hearing that statement, no cure for mental health repeatedly began to bother me, being that we had a severely mentally ill inmate that I was very familiar with in our administrative lockup unit at the time.

This individual had numerous assaults on staff, along with

suicide attempts. You were at risk every time you had to deal with this inmate for any reason. He would do things like rub his feces all over himself and commit inappropriate sexual acts in front of female staff regularly. If for any reason they had to open his food port, he would reach out and aggressively grab them, with no intention of letting go. We had to do forced entries into his cell regularly to inject him with medication due to his out-of-control behavior.

So, while I was in the MHSDS class, to get a reaction, I asked, "What about reintroducing frontal lobotomy?" I asked the question based on an article that I had previously read that described the process of a laser-guided cut just above both eyeballs that would sever the frontal lobe where our aggression in the brain comes from. It would be virtually undetectable and would presumably eradicate violent behavior.

The article went on to say that the procedure would almost eliminate the person's need for medication, other than maybe a small dose should the patient become too docile. I am not necessarily a fan of frontal lobotomy by any means, and I am not an expert. I was just curious to see how the psychiatrist would answer the question.

The psychiatrist took the route of frontal lobotomy being a cruel and unusual punishment, rather than a mental health procedure. But I couldn't help but think, *What about his multiple victims, all the people he has already injured and assaulted and will injure in the future? And is it right to leave the inmate in his present condition being he was an obvious threat to himself and everyone else?*

The following day, as I was telling this story to another custody staff member, someone that I wasn't aware of was standing behind me. He stated, "I would have to agree with you, Sergeant." I turned around to realize that person was our institution's chief medical officer. The CMO went on to inform me how we are setting ourselves up for a future medical and mental health problem because the excessive amounts of medication issued to the mental health inmates have to be filtered through their liver and kidneys. Like any other drug, they will eventually cause long-term damage to their internal organs, along with having other potential harmful repercussions to the human body. I found his information to be very interesting and something I would have never considered without the knowledge of a medical doctor.

Being a correctional sergeant but also a pastor in an institutional setting, I couldn't help but go out of my way to bring up the idea of spiritual-based therapy to complement our treatment programs already in place with our mental health professionals. Just bringing up the subject would typically be intercepted with extreme negativity, anger, and disgust.

The most positive feedback that I ever received from a psychiatrist was his statement that if he deemed it necessary, then he would refer an inmate who requested religious counsel to the chapel services of his choice.

I have always had a soft spot for the mentally ill. So many seem to be entirely in a world all their own, so we ignore or pacify them because we have to. Our job or society says we need to, yet we seem so inclined to be content in leaving them that way.

Here is a bit of information that I thought was interesting, taken from an article in *Scientific American:*

Do People Only Use 10 Percent of Their Brains?

The average human brain weighs about three pounds. "There are people who have injured their brains or [have] had parts [of them] removed who still live fairly normal lives, but that is because the brain has a way of compensating and making sure that what's left takes over the activity." If it is possible for a mentally ill person with a brain injury or even part of their brain removed to live a fairly normal life, then who are we to refuse to offer the full extent of our resources to assist them back on a potential road to recovery?

LET THE SUFFERING SPEAK

Through the years as a pastor, teacher, and counselor, I have learned that many times the best course of action leading to proper counsel and treatment of an individual comes from listening to those suffering the issue or illness themselves. Here is an example:

I was assigned the lockup unit, or administrative segregation unit, for a few years. Inmates in the lockup unit needed to be segregated and separated from the general population inmates for several administrative reasons. It is kind of like being in jail inside the prison, locked in your cell normally for twenty-plus hours a day, with occasional liberty for showering and exercise. I worked the tier that housed the vast majority of the inmates in the MHSDS. Every two days or so, the inmates on the tier were allowed to take a shower. Although we did have groups of inmates that would shower as a group, the MHSDS inmates had to shower by themselves or be on "walk alone status" meaning that all their activities on the tier would be conducted alone and not in any group, due to their mental illness and unpredictable behavior.

During this process, I would take the opportunity to speak with the inmate who would be waiting his turn behind a gate outside the shower. I would have a conversation with the MHSDS inmates to get their opinion as to what they were experiencing and why. Our conversation would commence as follows:

"So, you're in the mental health quad?"
"Yes, I am."
"So why are you in that quad?"
"I hear voices in my head."
"Really? What do the voices tell you?"
"They tell me to hurt someone or hurt myself."
"Where do you think these voices come from?"
"Oh, I know they are demons; I just don't know how to get rid of them!"

Without exception, in my personal experience, every inmate that I asked that question answered it the same way or at least in a similar manner: "I know they are demons; I just don't know how to get rid of them!"

I am not a psychologist or a psychiatrist, but I have conducted plenty of counseling with people from all different walks of life in their best or their worst possible season of life and circumstances. And all my experience has revealed to me that we are all imperfect, flawed, and damaged in one way or another. We need to understand that no matter how far we advance in technology or intellect—rather from a psychological, sociological, or religious perspective—if God exists, we will never be able to envelop our heads around an infinite God, being we are only finite!

So, if there is something that we don't understand that seems to be from a religious viewpoint, we discredit and remove it altogether; however, if it's a viewpoint from our intellect or that of our predecessors, whether it makes any sense or not, we change the wording to reflect a "theory" and incorporate this theory into our practice indefinitely. I find this biased method completely irrational when we are contending with people's lives, their livelihoods, and quite possibly the complete inner healing of an entire human being, along with the restoration of their self-respect. I have witnessed and have firsthand experience with many individuals completely distraught and broken, empty of themselves but clinging on to their belief and relationship with God, which brings their only hope in their seemingly hopeless situation.

By the way, I am in no way attempting to undermine our current mental health program and therapy. What I am saying is that we have to get over our religious and intellectual dogmas and hang-ups to expand our horizons for the sake of the mentally ill—to make every effort to give them back a life of renewal and self-respect.

The following information was taken from an article on a website called Bible Reasons, written by Fritz Chery on April 5, 2018.

Our Hearts Are Desperately Sick

We are psychosomatic unities. We will never understand how sick the human heart is. The mind-body connection is so strong that a mere thought can create panic attacks and depression. A mere thought can create pain that was never there. A mere thought makes the pain worse. For those who struggle with this, know this is not your fault. We are all broken, and I believe all people have a mental illness.

We all struggle with our thoughts in one way or another. We all overthink things, and sometimes our hearts and our minds hinder us from doing certain things and being in certain positions. You are not alone in this. Our hearts and our minds affect us all in different ways. You can't solve the problem without knowing the problem, and the problem is that we're broken sinners.

I recently viewed a program on Netflix, called *Inside the World's Toughest Prisons*. Why retired prison guards watch programs like this is a mystery! Anyway, an episode in season two was on Belize Central Prison. The narrator was Raphael Rowe, a British reporter who spent twelve years in a British prison for a murder he didn't commit and was released. In this series, Raphael Rowe voluntarily became incarcerated to experience what the prison system was about from the inside as a prisoner. Raphael Rowe openly claimed no religious affiliation.

In the 1990s, the prison was completely out of control due to deplorable living conditions and levels of violence. It got to the point where the Belize government could no longer afford to feed the inmate population. In 2002, the Kolbe Foundation, a private nongovernment nonprofit agency made up of local people in business, took over the prison. They claimed to provide a secure, humane facility geared toward meaningful rehabilitation of inmates. They believed that God could be a positive influence on the inmate's lives. From the time the inmates were released in the morning, and throughout the day, Christian sermons and music were played audibly over the PA system, along with other fundamental Christian programs available to assist inmates who wanted to change their lives. The recidivism rate of Belize Central Prison started at 73 percent before the takeover of the Kolbe Foundation, and it has now dropped to an astounding 23 percent!

It appears there is a lot more to the idea that God could have a profound influence on a person's life, and in the prison system than we thought.

Truly my soul finds rest in God;
my salvation comes from him.
Truly he is my rock and my salvation;
he is my fortress, I will never be shaken. (Psalm 62:1–2)

So you are no longer a slave, but God's child; and since you are his child, God has made you also an heir. (Galatians 4:7)

The LORD gives strength to his people;
the LORD blesses his people with peace. (Psalm 29:11)

The LORD is my light and my salvation—
whom shall I fear?
The LORD is the stronghold of my life—
of whom shall I be afraid? (Psalm 27:1)

Give thanks to the LORD, for he is good;
his love endures forever. (1 Chronicles 16:34)

He gives power to the tired and worn out, and strength to the weak. (Isaiah 40:29) (TLB)

For his anger lasts only a moment,
but his favor lasts a lifetime;
weeping may stay for the night,
but rejoicing comes in the morning. (Psalm 30:5)

How precious it is, LORD, to realize that you are thinking about me constantly! I can't even count how many times a day your thoughts turn toward me. And

when I waken in the morning, you are still thinking
of me! (Psalms 139: 17-18) (TLB)

For I will forgive their wickedness
and will remember their sins no more. (Hebrews 8:12)

I waited patiently for the LORD;
he turned to me and heard my cry. (Psalm 40:1)

Where can I go from your Spirit?
Where can I flee from your presence?
If I go up to the heavens, you are there;
if I make my bed in the depths, you are there.
If I rise on the wings of the dawn,
if I settle on the far side of the sea,
even there your hand will guide me,
your right hand will hold me fast. (Psalm 139:7–10)

That is what is meant by the Scriptures which say that
no mere man has ever seen, heard, or even imagined
what wonderful things God has ready for those who
love the Lord. (1 Corinthians 2:9) (TLB)

For your love and kindness are better to me than life
itself. How I praise you! (Psalms 63:3) (TLB)

"For I know the plans I have for you," declares the
LORD, "plans to prosper you and not to harm you,
plans to give you hope and a future." (Jeremiah 29:11)

You will seek me and find me when you seek me with
all your heart. (Jeremiah 29:13)

See, GOD has come to save me! I will trust and not be
afraid, for the LORD is my strength and song; he is my
salvation. (Isaiah 12:2) (TLB)

Let us hold unswervingly to the hope we profess, for he who promised is faithful. (Hebrews 10:23)

"For my thoughts are not your thoughts,
neither are your ways my ways,"
declares the LORD.
"As the heavens are higher than the earth,
so are my ways higher than your ways
and my thoughts than your thoughts." (Isaiah 55:8–9)

The heart is deceitful above all things
and beyond cure.
Who can understand it? (Jeremiah 17:9)

For it is from within, out of a person's heart, that evil thoughts come—sexual immorality, theft, murder, adultery, greed, malice, deceit, lewdness, envy, slander, arrogance, and folly. All these evils come from inside and defile a person. (Mark 7:21–23)

Whoever conceals their sins does not prosper,
but the one who confesses and renounces them finds mercy. (Proverbs 28:13)

Above all else, guard your heart,
for everything you do flows from it. (Proverbs 4:23)

CHAPTER 5

CRIMINAL JUSTICE PERSONNEL, MILITARY, AND FIRST RESPONDERS— RESPECT, HONOR, AND DIGNITY

In this chapter, we will take an inside look at the life of a correctional officer from inside the institutional setting, as well as on the street. The reason that I focus on the title starting with criminal justice personnel, or specifically a correctional officer, I am very familiar with this career and subject—thirty years familiar, to be exact. Although this chapter addresses the stress and pressure associated with the life of a correctional custody officer, all the principles contained in this chapter are relevant to all law enforcement personnel, military, and first responders. I recognize that other law enforcement, military, and first responding personnel deal with very stressful situations in the scopes of their careers; however, I cannot speak directly to that fact, or the details, and be completely accurate because I have never walked in your shoes.

I believe the correctional custody officer's career is a bit unique in that most correctional officers don't just deal with a felon now and then; they deal with hundreds, if not thousands, every day. I realize that can be an advantage or disadvantage, but as we liked to say, "At least we know what clientele we were dealing with!"

Law enforcement officers, military, and first responding personnel walk up to vehicles or respond to home disturbances, crime scenes, and so forth, without having any idea what they are getting themselves into—or, for that matter, if the individuals involved are friends or foe! As Douglas MacArthur said, "It is the soldier who must suffer and bear the deepest wounds and scars of war." The conflict, hostilities, and combat that we have endured during our contractual obligation may have come in different packages. But the accumulation of where we acquired our foundation of respect, how we categorize people, and the adverse effects of PTSD and job-related stress are virtually identical. All of these principles and the information throughout this book pertain directly to you and your career. In many ways, our job, focus, and goals are tightly woven together similarly. All respect and honor are due to you and yours, and thank you for your commitment, dedication, and valiant service!

Like most people that are not at all familiar with the inner workings of the prison system, I was also extremely naive as to what went on inside the correctional facilities when I first started my career in the Department of Corrections. I remember part of my testing process, which happened to take place at a correctional facility. I looked out the window and observed inmates walking all around the outside of the facility grounds and wondered why these guys weren't behind the walls or fences. My perception derived mostly from what I saw on television: walking everywhere in single file, feeding on bread and water, wearing black-and-white striped jumpsuits with a ball and chain around their ankles, and so on. Now, this example was old news well before modern programs like MSNBC, and other live broadcasts gave the public a glimpse of the life of an inmate inside the prison walls.

The prison system consists of multiple custody levels, and the crime an inmate is convicted of will determine the level of custody required for incarceration. Most correctional facilities are a city within a city, containing all different walks of life from various backgrounds and social classes, different ethnicities, education levels, gangs, and street affiliations, attitudes, and personalities. A correctional officer may work a tower or gun walk position with limited inmate contact, or they can be in a position where you have hundreds, if not thousands, of inmates walking all around you for your entire shift. The one thing that you can count on is that all the inmate population, regardless of custody levels, are all convicted felons. Keeping this fact in mind as you conduct your duties as a correctional officer keeps you on high alert and is very stressful.

Being that we are on the topic of stress in a prison setting, I must make a statement as to the stress related to correctional peers, supervisors, and administrators. I have been told by many fellow corrections staff for years that they would rather deal with hundreds of incarnated inmates than have to put up with some of the supervisors' or administrators' nonsense. Although there are some amazing and fantastic people working in correctional facilities, dealing with small man's complex, huge egos, incompetence, favoritism for different reasons, and blatant maltreatment of staff members is all commonplace in a correctional setting. It can send your stress level soaring and bankrupt a staff member of their honor and dignity. You see, the idea of the type of person who would commit to a career in prison doesn't necessarily draw the best candidates regarding the character and behavior of recruits, and the progression of upward mobility in corrections sometimes brings out the worst in people.

The stress level around the inmates and other staff members inside the prison walls is usually very tense. The last thing that you want to do inside the prison walls is to illuminate the perception in any way that you are weak and lose respect; you have to try to be yourself and not phony but not let your guard down. Your life may be in shambles, with your kids out of control, your wife just leaving you, experiencing financial ruin, or whatever adverse conditions you are facing. As you proceed through the gate and onto the facility, you do your best to put on your game face and leave it all behind you. By the way, good luck with that!

It is extremely difficult, if not impossible, for any correctional staff member to leave their world behind and not take it inside the prison, just as much as it is difficult, if not impossible, to leave your prison life in prison and not take it home with you! And in either case, it wreaks havoc on the job and definitely with your home life and your health. My wife is a beautiful saint. Many times throughout my career, I wondered how she put up with my poor attitude and verbal aggression, due to my work-related stress and fatigue.

After thirty years of service, I have two stents in my chest, sciatica, tinnitus, and an injured lower back. I wake up numerous times almost every night from pain in my hips, back, shoulders, and legs due to these injuries. A majority of prison yards, housing units, and general areas are constructed of solid base materials that cannot be penetrated, such as concrete and asphalt. Inmates tend to do bad things in soft surfaces like dirt and grass. They bury weapons, drugs, hype kits, and other dangerous contraband items. Inmates quite often hide contraband in common areas for easy access when needed and to avoid having the item in their possession be detected by custody staff and possibly do additional time on their sentence. Walking and running (responding to emergencies) on these hard surfaces for many years with heavy equipment on my hips and back has proven to be a substantial contributing factor to the work-related injuries that I have sustained, as well as advancement in my sleep disorder.

But stress associated with a job in corrections also causes some strange psychological and social behavioral changes in an officer as well. The idea that you can take a correctional officer out of prison, but you can't take the prison out of the correctional officer is an undeniable truism.

SOMEONE YOU'RE NOT

Quite a few years ago, I was attending a Bible study, with a couple of other correctional officers in attendance. In one of our conversations, the pastor conducting the study made a comment that has stuck with me through the years, one that I can never forget. He stated that the scariest thing about our job is that it forces us to be "someone that you are not." He went on to say that if you have a bad day, you have to pretend you didn't—if you are not a combative or physically violent natured person—it doesn't matter because you will be confronted with situations in which you have to take action, you don't have a choice. You have to, in a sense, go into a survival mode to function in your working environment, whether it's who you are or not; having to be put in this situation regularly is potentially damaging to you as a person in many different ways. Throughout my career in corrections, I have seen this principle disclosed in the life of staff members on many occasions.

My youngest daughter was quite an athlete and participated in a variety of sports growing up. I was her coach for quite a few of her athletic endeavors. During the season, I would quite often try to get the parents involved by speaking to the parents in a group either before, during, or after practice. I had a great time getting to know and speak with the parents of the team members, and in time, conversations would become quite personal, where one of the parents would ask me what I do for a living or where I work. When I would mention that I worked for the state at the prison, parents would often stop in their tracks and stare at me with a blank, serious look on their faces, before asking, "Aren't you supposed to be mean and hateful, like everyone else who works out there?" From that point, they would usually go on to tell a story about a neighbor, friend, or relative who worked at the prison and describe their bizarre or even brutal behavior.

Along with parents, I have heard these same or similar statements verbalized by car salespersons, real estate agents, school officials, and beyond. "Aren't you supposed to be a mean and hateful, like everyone else who works out there?"

In some cases, I would think, Yeah, it makes sense that that particular officer they are referring to does quite often display dirty, mean, and hateful behavior. But more often than not, statements like that would catch me off guard, being that I would be familiar with the staff member referred to and their demeanor on the job, and I would have never guessed that they would act in such a manner like that outside of work! Not to make excuses for anybody's poor behavior, but as I would reflect on the prison system's negative work environment and the nonsense that a custody correctional employee would have to put up with daily, it made sense as to how the degrading and inappropriate behavior would eventually come about.

The stress level and long, strange hours that a correctional officer or other law enforcement officials work affect us differently. However, with as much counseling and coaching that I have done from the inside, there is one particular behavior that seems to surface more frequently than others: *isolation*. Because of what we do and whom we have to deal with at work, it quite often leads us to desire isolation, perhaps to be all alone in a dark room or hide in the corner of the room in a comfortable chair after work and tune everything and everyone out. The problem is that it would be inclusive of our wife, kids, and all those closest to us that mean the most. I recently spoke with a correctional officer's ex-wife as we were busy working on an outdoor project together with some other people. She spoke to me about her ex-husband's behavior. "He would come home from work mean and angry. The kids and I wouldn't have anything to do with him because he was so mean. The animals in the house were even afraid of him; he treated us all like we were dogs."

I have counseled with many fellow correctional officers and law enforcement officials, trying to help them pick up the pieces of their broken lives, and the shattered remnants of their family after divorce had left them emotionally bankrupt and dejected. To date, very few perceived the marital breakdown or how their behavior was affecting their family, either too stressed out or caught up to consider any constructive changes. They never saw or understood the turmoil that was erupting right in their own homes, until it was too late.

Here is some information based on studies done at Washington State University—Health and Medicine Research—that might help shed some light on the negative behavior progress in the life of a correctional officer.

- Prison employees work under an almost constant state of threat to their personal safety, and about a quarter of them routinely experience serious threats to themselves or their families.
- Almost half have witnessed coworkers being seriously injured by inmates.
- More than half have seen an inmate die or have encountered an inmate who recently died.
- The vast majority have dealt with inmates who were recently beaten or sexually assaulted.
- Prison workers have some of the highest rates of sleep disorders and physical health issues of all US workers.

Through the years, the Department of Corrections has made meager attempts to deal with the ongoing problem of employees' stress and trauma through such programs as EAP and EPTP. EAP (Employee Assistance Program) offers employees free counseling sessions to help staff deal with their life and job-related struggles. EPTP (Employee Post Trauma Program) consists of a group of staff members trained in helping employees deal with post-trauma, normally after a serious incident occurred.

Before these programs existed, we had to find a way to deal with our post-trauma on our own. Our post-trauma would normally consist of a group of staff members who were involved in the incident but not severely injured, meeting in a big room to discuss the details. We would normally try to find something that occurred during the incident that was unusual or funny, so we could get a good laugh in to ease the pressure a bit. There always seemed to be a segment that would bring about humor once we took a little time to debrief and talk about the circumstances that took place.

I still remember my first exposure to our old-school employee post-trauma. I mentioned an all-out brawl between custody staff and the Cuban inmates, back in the early 1980s, in Chapter Three. After the brawl had taken place and the inmates involved were locked up, all of the custody staff involved met in the visiting room to debrief, assess injuries, and try to calm down.

There was a certain lieutenant who happened to be the watch commander that evening. We will call him Lieutenant Dan (no pun intended for you *Forrest Gump* fans). Lieutenant Dan was old to be in the prison setting, I'm guessing mid- to late sixties. Lieutenant Dan was very proud ex-military, and everything about him reflected his dedication and loyalty. He wore his class A uniform every day, neatly pressed, with razor-sharp creases. The bill of his class A hat and his work shoes were always spit shined with a mirror finish; he always looked sharp and ready for action!

In the middle of our debriefing session after the incident, in walked Lieutenant Dan, he was furious. His uniform was torn, and his shoes were scuffed. He was holding his hat in his hand and had scratches on his face and hands. He kept repeating himself over and over, yelling as loud as he could, "Who in the **** kept throwing me in the bushes?!" Everybody in the room hesitated for just a moment and then started laughing hysterically.

During the incident, Lieutenant Dan had come running out of the watch commander's office with the full intention of jumping right in the middle of the melee. Right in front of the watch office, a hedge of bushes separated the walkway from the grass area. Some staff members felt he was too old and would get hurt, so every time Lieutenant Dan would get close to the altercation, someone would grab him from behind, spin him around, and push him into the bushes. Lieutenant Dan wasn't very happy having to fight his way out of the bushes every couple of minutes! But that's what took place and serves as a reflection as my first exposure to one of our old-school employee post-trauma debriefing sessions.

In my estimation, female correctional officers in a male prison get a terrible, if not the worst, end of the deal, frequently turning into a completely different person from whom they were when they started. One of the female officers stressed her impression to me once when she stated, "As a female officer, you have no choice but to have these guys around you all day long, staring, gawking, no matter how pretty you are or not. What you think they are thinking about?"

I remember being with my family on vacation at Universal Studios Hollywood. We were all having a great time and decided that we wanted to experience the studio tour. On the way to the studio tour, you descend a whole hillside of concrete stairs, cascading from the top of the hill to the bottom. About halfway down the hill, an alarm went off, and I took off running as fast as I could, dodging and weaving in and out of people for a couple of flights before I caught myself and just had to laugh. One of the warehouses at the bottom of the stairwell has an alarm that sounds just like the loud, obnoxious alarms inside the prison. Instinctively, without a thought, even though on vacation with the family, my mind said to respond! This instinctive action wasn't the first or the last time that I responded to an alarm outside the prison and had to take some time to explain myself.

HITTING BOTTOM

Working in a correctional setting, you question every move an inmate makes, every word an inmate says, and you try to locate ulterior motives behind every action, no matter how routine or trivial they may appear. You find yourself being suspicious of every inmate you encounter, maintaining both a professional and interpersonal relationship with them, and at the same time thinking, *This inmate could become violent and potentially seriously assault me at any given moment.* This observation would be a brief glimpse into the mind of a correctional officer on a routine basis!

The stress level mentioned above would describe the stress associated with a correctional officer's job daily. To add to an already stress-filled situation, the environment inside most correctional facilities is ever-changing and extremely unpredictable. There are outside CDCR buses and other transportation units relocating inmates in and out of different facilities every day. Inside the correctional facilities, inmate movement is also conducted in the form of bed, yard, and cell moves. This repetitive movement causes a continual substitution and the potential for turmoil among the inmate population.

I spent the majority of my career on level two and three facilities. In this level of custody, inmates have plenty of freedom to spend on the open yard, outside their housing units, to partake in yard activities, to converse or conflict, during daylight hours and into the evening well after daylight hours. Malice and menacing are common during yard activities, making the prison yard continually infused with the potential for upheaval among the inmate population.

Sometimes there are signs of tension in the yard that would indicate a problem. Large groups of inmates congregated together for protection because they are at war with another ethnicity or gang. Or inmates dressed for "combat" by wearing multiple clothing layers with heavy jackets to try to shield them from stabbing instruments used during an altercation. Other times there is no warning at all. An emergency alarm sounds or a radio call is transmitted, and your routine day erupts into utter chaos. You immediately respond to the affected area to access the situation and offer your assistance. You normally have no idea what kind of havoc or situation you will be running into—melee, riot, staff assault, cutter, hanger, weapons involved. All these haunting thoughts and many more echo and race through your mind as you respond with all diligence.

It appears that more research seems to be surfacing regarding the lives and job-related stress associated with a correctional officer's career and the catastrophic cumulative effects on a CO's health. It's a long time coming being that the National Criminal Justice Reference Service, the *Denver Post*, and other resources state that the national life span average is seventy-seven, whereas a correctional officer's life span plummets to fifty-nine. There always seems to be a lot of talk about prison reform, but correctional officers are being left out of the conversation!

According to a recent study featured in *Force Science News*, corrections officers **experience PTSD symptoms at a war-zone level**. PTSD, which stands for *post-traumatic stress disorder,* affects individuals who have seen shocking events, such as warfare or sexual assault. Its symptoms kick in within three months of the traumatic incident, but they may also occur years later. These usually include extreme fear and anxiety, nightmares, chills, heart palpitations, flashbacks, loss of motivation, feelings of guilt, and more.

Many officers suffer in silence, telling themselves that they need to be strong, so the actual numbers are significantly higher. Even those who don't develop PTSD experience high-stress levels and burnout. Researchers believe that traumatic events, such as being injured on the job, receiving threats, and witnessing inmates attempting suicide, play a major role in the onset of this disorder. It's not uncommon for jail guards to see inmates killing each other, engaging in large-scale fights, or setting their cells on fire. Some prisoners will harm themselves or commit suicide. Hepatitis, AIDS and other infectious diseases are common in a prison environment—and correctional staff are exposed to these risks on a daily basis.

The violence in prisons haunts guards' private lives. They begin to treat their family and friends like they treat convicts, lose their trust in people, and feel threatened daily.

PTSD, DEPRESSION, SUICIDE, AND DIVORCE ARE HIGHEST AMONG CORRECTIONAL OFFICERS

Here are a few highlights from a recent article posted on May 21, 2018, by *Armorupnow,* written by Brian Dawe, executive director of the American Correctional Officer Intelligence Network and former Massachusetts state correctional officer.

On average, ten correctional officers die in the line of duty every year, whereas 156 correctional officers take their own lives every year. The cumulative negative affects this job has on our health is devastating. For every officer that dies in the line of duty, fifteen take their own lives: "Over time, negative work experiences and resulting psychological distress may have a cumulative impact that shapes personality adversely and causes individuals to develop a more pervasively negative outlook."

Do you jump when the phone rings, even when you're off the job? Is your first reaction to your children's request no, regardless of what they're asking? Do you sit with your back to the wall in order to watch ingress and egress points? Do you feel emotions well up in you far above what the situation warrants? Are you frequently tired and consuming more alcohol than before? Are you often asked by family and friends if everything is all right? Have you stopped listening? Do you seek more solitude and alone time?

In short, correctional officers have a 39 percent higher suicide rate, PTSD rates ten times higher than the general population, a divorce rate that's 20 percent higher than the national average, and heart disease affects us at a rate that is 50 percent higher than any other occupation. These statistics are sobering, even more so because they are so underreported.

We walk around with our arms pumped up and our chests out and say to ourselves, "I got this," when in reality, *no,* you don't "have it," but in time, overwhelming stats dictate that it will probably get you! Stress, PTSD, heart disease, and these other mentioned ailments are silent but violent killers! They are no respecters of pride, status, or personality, and they don't always give you a warning until you are infected and never even saw it coming. These devastating wounds are not visible from the outside.

I know that there are many out there who are in the same position I was. It's not like you have the option to simply change your career overnight and do something different or less stressful. You are not automatically predestined to be a product of your work environment, surroundings, or the adverse conditions that so often accompany your stressful carrier. But if you don't have a life outside your job, chances are you will! Because the hardest prison to escape is in our own mind.

There are healthy habits and programs that you can incorporate into your personal lives that will defer or even eliminate these stats from ever becoming part of your personal story. Be intentional to formulate some non-work-related healthy activities.

Here are just a few suggestions:

- Get involved in a church. No, I don't only say that because I am a pastor! In a good, healthy church, you and the whole family can get involved, which does wonders for your personal and family health, strengthening that family bond.
- Walk and talk with family, friends, or both, perhaps at a park, school, or after mapping out multiple trails.
- Kayak, paddleboard, or go fishing.
- Take up a hobby or pursue an interest.
- Work out at home or join a gym and work out. Exercise is essential for stress relief, whether swimming, running, Pilates … or whatever!
- Listen to some soothing, relaxing music.
- Drink tea, or another soothing non-alcoholic beverage, which will assist in those negative stats not becoming part of your personal life story!
- Forgive: when you choose not to forgive and get over it, no matter how bad the circumstances, you remain the victim!

- Accept people for who or what they are! You only drive yourself mad when you get angry and judgmental, disapproving of others. And it doesn't change a thing.
- Volunteer in your child's classroom, whatever the teacher would have you to help with, class projects, field trips, and so forth.
- Go to the school office and request to take your child out of school and take them out for a special lunch. They will remember it forever!
- Make an agreement with your spouse that when you get home from work and change clothes, you are to be left alone in an isolated area like your bedroom for thirty minutes or so to change clothes, shut your eyes, and relax before getting involved in your home life duties and responsibilities.
- Have open talk family meetings with your spouse and kids, asking them for their honest opinion: Are things okay? What needs to change? What do we need to do differently? Ask them open-end questions and listen to their responses.
- Above all, do not let your pride or ego get the best of you. If you need outside professional help, then get it! It's available to you and is normally free of charge, due to your high-stress occupation.

Most of the greatest people that I have ever met in my life, I met in prison, inclusive of staff and inmates. One thing that I noticed through the years is that the prison setting poses the opportunity for someone to get *"real."* The bizarre, violent, obscured, stressful, and downright gross incidents and issues that a person will encounter has the potential to make a person take a look deep inside and do some serious evaluation of one's life. A prison is a great place for a person to hit bottom, both mentally and spiritually. I like to think that once a person truly hits bottom, there is only one way to look—and that is up! Based on the information above on stress and PTSD, my hope is that my fellow corrections, law enforcement, military personnel, and first responders everywhere will do just that: *look up*! Looking up will help us understand and realize where the true restoration and support of their respect, honor, and dignity generates.

Speaking of coming to terms with the truth about who you are and where you are going, I can honestly say there are probably a handful of inmates that I have had interactions with throughout my career whom I would feel totally at ease with having as a next-door neighbor.

One, in particular, was an inmate clerk during my tenure as an outside community work crew sergeant. We will call him Mike. Mike told me his story, and I will never forget it. He explained to me that he came from a single-parent home. His mother had passed when he was young, so his dad raised him alone. Right after graduating from high school, Mike wanted to attend a university. Although his dad was very wealthy, he told his son, "Mike, I found a way to do it on my own, and you are going to do the same. I'm not paying any money for your college education." Mike went on to tell me that he was an avid scuba diver at the Channel Islands, an area that I was familiar with off the coast of California, in the Pacific Ocean. He was also a part-owner of a large boat with two other friends, and they frequently used it to accommodate their fishing and diving excursions.

One day a man approached the young men at their boat dock, and he explained to them that they could utilize their vessel to pick up a package for him across the border of Mexico, just a few times a year, and make a lot of money. Mike now had his way to "do it on his own" and pay for his college education. His new way of doing things paid for his entire university education. The problem was that after he graduated, he thought, *Now I am going to work a regular nine-to-five job when I can do this a couple of times a year and make a whole lot more money, live comfortably, with plenty of free time to do what I want?*

Mike and his counterparts were arrested for drug trafficking, and he was serving his time in the state prison. He said that it gave him a lot of time to slow down and think about how stupid a choice he made being young and dumb. That if he didn't get arrested, he would be fish food on the bottom of the ocean somewhere. He then made a statement that I will never forget: "So when I was arrested, I wasn't so much arrested as I was rescued from my stupidity!"

There are those occurrences when the system proves effective, and this was one of them.

Trusting Jesus and taking Him into prison or on patrol will make all the difference in your world and career. I know because it did in mine! I didn't get out unscathed. I mentioned my injuries from stress and probably caring about people too much! I'm not trying to preach to you, but I have always prided myself on being real with people. I have spent too many years attempting to help fellow staff members pick up the broken pieces of their lives, not to tell you the truth. I have experienced the stress and drama from both sides—with and without knowing Christ personally—and there is no substitute even close to His divine presence in my personal life and during my tenure in this high-stress work environment.

> For we do not have a high priest who is unable to empathize with our weaknesses, but we have one who has been tempted in every way, just as we are—yet he did not sin. Let us then approach God's throne of grace with confidence, so that we may receive mercy and find grace to help us in our time of need. (Hebrews 4:15–16)

> I will give them an undivided heart and put a new spirit in them; I will remove from them their heart of stone and give them a heart of flesh. (Ezekiel 11:19)

> For God says, "Your cry came to me at a favorable time, when the doors of welcome were wide open. I helped you on a day when salvation was being offered." Right now, God is ready to welcome you. Today he is ready to save you.
> (2 Corinthians 6:2) (TLB)

> But you, LORD, are a shield around me,
> my glory, the One who lifts my head high. (Psalm 3:3)

Don't you realize how patient he is being with you? Or don't you care? Can't you see that he has been waiting all this time without punishing you, to give you time to turn from your sin? His kindness is meant to lead you to repentance. (Romans 2:4) (TLB)

Come to me, all you who are weary and burdened, and I will give you rest. Take my yoke upon you and learn from me, for I am gentle and humble in heart, and you will find rest for your souls. (Matthew 11:28–29)

I lift up my eyes to the mountains—
where does my help come from?
My help comes from the LORD,
the Maker of heaven and earth. (Psalm 121:1)

May the God of hope fill you with all joy and peace as you trust in him, so that you may overflow with hope by the power of the Holy Spirit. (Romans 15:13)

Do not be anxious about anything, but in every situation, by prayer and petition, with thanksgiving, present your requests to God. And the peace of God, which transcends all understanding, will guard your hearts and your minds in Christ Jesus. (Philippians 4:6-7)

But those who hope in the LORD
will renew their strength.
They will soar on wings like eagles;
they will run and not grow weary,
they will walk and not be faint. (Isaiah 40:31)

CHAPTER 6

OUR ROAD THROUGH SAMARIA

A few years back, I was leading a young adult Bible study. As the study progressed through the Gospels, the question came up: "Why Samaria?" Why are the Samaritan people and the geographic area of Samaria used so many times in key parables describing crucial matters? The woman at the well was a Samaritan, the parable of the Good Samaritan, the Samaritan leper—why Samaritan?

In the Bible, Jesus demonstrated that He was not ashamed to violate manmade traditions. He touched lepers even though they were considered unclean. He talked with Samaritan women, even though it was forbidden. So, we took a couple of weeks to find out the answer to this question: "Why Samaria?" This is what we discovered.

Samaria was located in the central region, or heart, of the ancient nation of Israel. The land of Israel was taken over and occupied by a host of different world empires through the centuries, including Assyria, Babylon, Persia, Greece, and Rome, just to name a few. The leaders of the occupying nation at the time would quite often exile the key figureheads, and people of significance to their own country. They would then leave a group or even a large number of the local population in the land and assign a leader of their own to govern the nation, who would be loyal to the king or leader of the occupying nation. It is recorded that during the Assyrian occupation, the king of Assyria alone sent peoples from Cutha, Ava, Hamath, and Sepharvaim to inhabit Samaria.

Through the years, Samaria was a sort of a dumping ground for various peoples and ethnicities. These foreigners intermarried with the Israelite population that was still in and around Samaria. The results were clusters of several kinds of people from all different lifestyles with mixed bloodlines, and due to the Samaritan population's mixing of bloodlines, the Samaritans were considered half-breeds and worse—people universally despised, the worst of the human race.

Many Jews of that period would have no dealings with them. Jews who were traveling from Judea to Galilee, or vice versa, would cross over the Jordan River and avoid Samaria by going through Transjordan, traveling many additional miles out of their way. They would then cross back over the river again once they had reached their destination rather than contaminate themselves by passing through Samaritan territory.

I love the fact that Jesus used the Samaritans so many times in His examples and parables while teaching the people. It was the ultimate way of dispensing the truth that all people are equal in God's eyes, regardless of ethnicity, gender, or status. Jesus makes this very clear by His emphasis on Samaria, that every human being is substantial and significant.

At some time in our adult lives, everyone needs to take a personal journey through Samaria. Take the journey to Samaria as many times as necessary and remain there as long as it takes to allow this purging process to have its full impact in your life. Now, this may seem a bit odd to you, so please let me explain.

Your journey through Samaria is not physical; consider it an exercise in wellness. A wellness journey is not unusual. Every day we journey in our minds to find that place of peace and refuge, to escape the routine drudgery of our daily grind and attempt to escape our present condition or the circumstances.

I had a dentist a few years back who had a great idea that always helped me get through the "dental experience." When it was time to get busy in my mouth after those wonderful Novocain injections had taken effect, the chair would recline way back. *You know what I'm talking about!* You have to stare straight up at the ceiling. The dentist had strategically mounted a picture in the perfect position on the ceiling to look at while in this reclined position. The picture was of a beautiful tropical beach scene. It was a warm summer day, with powdery white beach sand, stunning turquoise-blue clear water, a cluster of palm trees in the corner, and one single beach chair with an umbrella overhead and an ice chest right beside it. As the mouth mirror probes and rotary drill were doing a job on my grill, it didn't take a lot of imagination to figure out where I had escaped to in my mind!

Your excursion in Samaria is no day at the beach. It is subjective, personalized, individual, cultural, and situational. It causes abundant fear, along with immense freedom. In your Samaria, you lose all your prior prejudice and preconceived notions about other people. You will encounter people from many different geographical areas around the world, an abundance of multicolored faces, ethnicities, and cultures that you know very little to nothing about. You lose your ego and gang status; nobody is impressed with your tattoos or your physical physique, intellect, religious intolerance, or parental and political influence. There is no pressure to measure up; none of it matters anymore. You are left stripped of all previous identity, barren and empty; you identify your preconceived notions and prejudice thoughts, but you leave them in your Samaria.

In your Samaria, you must deal with positive change and stare diversity in the face, surrendering any pretense and defense mechanisms that have made you comfortable in the past. You gain an understanding that you were not created to be a thief or a drug addict, controlled by your pride, ego, intellect, or the amount of money or material possessions you own. If you are honest with yourself, you start your journey through Samaria one person, but you are not the same person when you come out!

It is now time for your journey through Samaria. I recommend that you go somewhere quiet if possible, where you can be alone and uninterrupted for at least an hour or so. And so, your journey begins!

You have traveled far and long to finally arrive at the starting point of your life lesson through Samaria, and you are exhausted. Your driver doesn't speak to you at all in the vehicle, but as you arrive at your destination, he gives you two instructions: gather intelligence and survive. Your first thought: *Gather intelligence and survive? What does he mean by that?* As you turn back toward the vehicle to ask the driver for further clarification, he abruptly pulls away and is gone. You have been dropped off at the entrance to the trailhead into Samaria, all alone with no provisions. There is no turning back! Behind you lie miles and miles of massive dunes of sand. Nothing but a hot, dry, barren, uninhabited desert. You must now enter your Samaria for your mere survival. Your objective is to be neutral and unbiased. You are not to show unfair favoritism for one person over another based on your prejudice or personal feelings.

Initially, you are hesitant but curious with anticipation about a new experience. But as you enter your Samaria, it was not at all what you were expecting. You have entered right in the middle of the market street area, where a majority of the Samaritan people congregate at the end of the day. You are in the direct sunlight. It is scorching, hot and loud, people are everywhere around you. All this commotion soon forces you to be on your guard. Your emotions and intensity run high—all these people, this sea of multicolored faces, staring directly at you, speaking multiple unknown languages. You assume they are talking about you, but you can't understand a word that they are saying. Nobody is familiar, and at this point, nothing is predictable.

You remain on high alert and vigilant as your heart rate and blood pressure increase, the heat is intense, so you keep walking. You are trapped in your overwhelming thoughts and feelings while wondering who you can approach and what you should say. What are these people's intentions? What are they thinking? You feel acute stress as your heart beats even faster. You are now at an alarm stage and mentally terrified!

Just about this time, your mind tells you to arm yourself or run as fast as you possibly can. Reality then sets in, and you now realize that everyone here is just an ordinary person going about their everyday business. They are all staring at you because they are wondering the same things you are! They are curious to know who you are, where you came from, what brings you to Samaria. Are you a friend or foe? You are now finally able to drop your guard, and you are approachable.

One of the Samaritan gentlemen standing just inside a shade-covered shelter motions for you to come over to his location, and join their posse of numerous integrated people as they share their stories of fear, triumph, family, friends, and whatever else comes to mind. You accept his gracious invitation. Everyone is curious to find out who you are and hear all your amazing stories as you enjoy an ice-cold drink and break bread together, enjoying each other's company. You are smiling and laughing, engaging your newfound friends in a meaningful heart-to-heart conversation. You begin to explore and appreciate new cultures with some great people, expanding your horizons with a completely different mindset, approach, and attitude. You are taking part in an amazing experience that you never thought would have ever been possible.

Congratulations! You not only survived your journey through Samaria, but you also prospered greatly from the whole excursion. By the way, do you still remember your preconceived notions and prejudiced thoughts that were part of you when you first entered your journey through Samaria? Great! Leave them there in Samaria permanently as instructed; do not take them with you on the way out!

Allowing yourself the opportunity to look deep inside and finally get "real" about your preconceived notions and prejudices toward other people can trigger concern or anxiety or be downright painful. Exhibiting this type of behavior toward other people is not always a choice on our part. Normally it is a subconscious act based on a variety of stimuli, such as false ideology, the influence of media, hearsay, and our friends, family, or parents.

Your journey through Samaria is an exercise in wellness that is necessary to let go of these hindering issues that so easily beset us so that you can figure out who you are and what is most important in your life. Our road through Samaria will help us fulfill our responsibility to treat others with respect and dignity.

SUCCESSFUL OR FAITHFUL

We are all bombarded by people, television, and voices assuring us that the good life consists of amassing wealth, accumulating personal power, achieving success, and forging the kinds of relationships that we desire. But to even perceive for a moment that earthly blessings such as money and power in and of themselves will bring lasting fulfillment and joy into our lives is complete folly. Throughout my lifetime, I have seen and experienced plenty of people that fell victim to this vicious trap, only to grow old and lonely, wishing they would have lived their lives differently. Here are a few examples.

While assigned as the watch sergeant inside the institution, I would receive many different phone calls from different people outside the facility. Over time, I received numerous calls from retired or former administrative prison officials who seemed to have a serious problem letting go, understanding that now they didn't hold their position anymore, that their previously held position and influence didn't matter. They would quite often call and state their formerly held position, demanding that I give them some information or connect them to a certain person. I would have to remind them that I had no way to identify who they were and that now they were just civilians, like any other caller. That reality would be difficult for them to come to terms with being that their identity and livelihood were so immersed in the previous position they held.

I recently spoke with a friend who had just conversed with a mutual acquaintance of ours who had retired as one of the correctional institution's wardens. This individual was an extremely arrogant person who always had to be right and didn't seem to care about anybody but himself. He had been retired for a few years and came to a grim reality. While he held his position as warden, he could treat people terribly and get away with it. People would treat him as if he was someone special or important because it was job-related, so the employees in his sphere of influence were obligated to treat him with seeming honor and respect due to his position.

But now that he is retired, all those coworkers and so-called friends have nothing to gain from him anymore, so they go on with life and act as if he doesn't even exist. They have nothing to do with him; no one calls, comes over to his house, or pays him any attention. He told my friend something that I never thought he would ever say. He said that his number one regret in life *and* his career was that he wished he would have treated people better. People respected or tolerated him because of his position, but not him as a person, and that can be a very damaging truth when reality sets in, and we have to face it.

A principle we often lose sight of is that faithfulness is more important than success, doing what's right and right by people, regardless of the circumstances, is crucial. Greatness is measured but by our determination to use the power and influence God gives us, however great or small, to positively affect our lives and the lives of those in our sphere of influence through meaningful and positive relationships.

In life, we face situations that seem impossible: a problematic marriage, wrestling with our pasts, contending with our seemingly grim futures, our life in a world that sometimes despises the things we cherish most. We wonder if anything good can result from our current situation or circumstances. None of us can preclude the possibility that our circumstances will radically change for the better, but we can hold onto the hope of the one who holds the future in his hands. God never requires us to be successful, only faithful.

OUR MOST IMMINENT NEED

Throughout our society and the world abroad, we have epidemic levels of people searching and striving to find that thing, experience, or substance that will fulfill the human heart and bring about lasting comfort and significance. God only knows the heights and depths that we will go to reach that goal of fulfillment. As we run the gauntlet of life, we all have to come to the same reality. No matter who you are, and regardless of your race, creed, or color, we all suffer from the same prominent desire to be truly loved and fully accepted. To be truly loved and fully accepted is the most basic need of the human heart.

Nothing in human beings' lives has such lasting and fatal effects as the experience of not being completely loved and fully accepted.

When I am not truly loved and fully accepted, something in me is twisted and broken. Infant and children who are not welcome could potentially be scarred for the rest of their lives.

According to an article titled "Bonding Is Essential for Normal Infant Development," by the UC Davis Medical Center, the importance of bonding with the primary caregiver cannot be overestimated. Failure to do so profoundly affects future development and the ability to form healthy relationships as an adult.

A September 2012 article in *The Guardian* titled "Why Secure Early Bonding Is Essential for Babies" states that secure early bonding is the difference between the baby that grows up a secure, emotionally capable adult, and a baby that will become a depressive, anxious child who will not cope well with life's ups and downs. In the most difficult cases, this baby is more likely to later experience criminality, substance abuse, or depressive problems.

The previous articles only dealt with the infant or child. How about the adverse effects on a student who feels like an outcast from his teacher and has issues learning? Or people who do not feel accepted by their colleagues on the job? In the life history of convicted felons or prisoners, evidence would conclude that somewhere along life's path, they went astray because no one loved and accepted them.

Some people are driven toward becoming workaholics, always striving for acceptance, and never feeling satisfied that they measure up. Others become caught up in withdrawal and apathy, or even turn angry or hostile, and the list goes on and on. People who don't come to grips with the lack of love and acceptance in their lives generally vent in a variety of different ways. They typically either turn their pain inward, which leads to anxiety, depression, emotional withdrawal, and detachment—or outward, carrying a chip on their shoulders. Often mean and angry at life and other people in general. But either way, their pain, and sorrows escalate because they don't face the painful truth, regarding their lack of true love and full acceptance.

To be loved and accepted means those people who are an intrinsic part of my life give me a feeling of self-respect, a feeling that I am valuable. They are glad that I am who I am, and although there is a need for growth, I am not forced or locked into my past or the present. I am given room and encouraged to develop and outgrow the mistakes of my past. Acceptance liberates everything in me— only when I am loved in that deep sense of complete acceptance can I become myself. Every one of us is born with a whole lot of potential, but unless these potentialities are drawn out through love and acceptance, they will remain dormant.

Our greatest objective in life, to be truly loved and fully accepted as human beings, is inescapable. However, our love and acceptance for each other always seem to be integrated with strings attached: "I truly love you until …" or "I fully accept you if …." So, I guess the question that we have to ask ourselves is, where do we go to find love without condition, or "unconditional" love and acceptance? No gadgets, no gizmos, and, most of all, no strings attached!

THE WOMAN AT THE WELL

Now he had to go through Samaria. So, he came to a town in Samaria called Sychar, near the plot of ground Jacob had given to his son Joseph. Jacob's well was there, and Jesus, tired as he was from the journey, sat down by the well. It was about noon. When a Samaritan woman came to draw water, Jesus said to her, "Will you give me a drink?" (His disciples had gone into the town to buy food.) The Samaritan woman said to him, "You are a Jew, and I am a Samaritan woman. How can you ask me for a drink?" (For Jews do not associate with Samaritans.) (John 4:4–9)

THE PARABLE OF THE GOOD SAMARITAN

In reply, Jesus said, "A man was going down from Jerusalem to Jericho when he was attacked by robbers. They stripped him of his clothes, beat him and went away, leaving him half dead. A priest happened to be going down the same road, and when he saw the man, he passed by on the other side. So too, a Levite, when he came to the place and saw him, passed by on the other side. But a Samaritan, as he traveled, came where the man was; and when he saw him, he took pity on him. He went to him and bandaged his wounds, pouring on oil and wine. Then he put the man on his own donkey, brought him to an inn and took care of him. The next day he took out two denarii and gave them to the innkeeper. 'Look after him,' he said, 'and when I return, I will reimburse you for any extra expense you may have.'" (Luke 10:30–35)

THE SAMARITAN LEPER

Now on his way to Jerusalem, Jesus traveled along the border between Samaria and Galilee. As he was going into a village, ten men who had leprosy met him. They stood at a distance and called out in a loud voice, "Jesus, Master, have pity on us! When he saw them, he said, "Go, show yourselves to the priests." And as they went, they were cleansed. One of them, when he saw he was healed, came back, praising God in a loud voice. He threw himself at Jesus's feet and thanked him—and he was a Samaritan. (Luke 17:11–15)

You are my hiding place;
you will protect me from trouble
and surround me with songs of deliverance. (Psalm 32:7)

For I am convinced that neither death nor life, neither angels nor demons, neither the present nor the future, nor any powers, neither height nor depth, nor anything else in all creation, will be able to separate us from the love of God that is in Christ Jesus our Lord. (Romans 8:38–39)

Where can I go from your Spirit?
Where can I flee from your presence?
If I go up to the heavens, you are there;
if I make my bed in the depths, you are there.
If I rise on the wings of the dawn,
if I settle on the far side of the sea,
even there your hand will guide me,
your right hand will hold me fast. (Psalm 139:7–10)

In him and through faith in him we may approach God with freedom and confidence. (Ephesians 3:12)

The following Scripture, recorded in Psalm 51, was part of a reaction from King David after the prophet Nathan approached him regarding his dreadful acts. King David had committed adultery and murder. King David was referred to by God as a "man after God's own heart" before these repulsive acts and even after. Even though King David did these terrible things, he had to be right and get right with God—and not without punishment and consequences—but his relationship was restored. That's what made King David a "man after God's own heart."

Have mercy on me, O GOD,
according to your unfailing love;
according to your great compassion
blot out my transgressions.
Wash away all my iniquity
and cleanse me from my sin. (Psalm 51:1–2)

It is a broken spirit you want—remorse and penitence.
A broken and a contrite heart, O GOD, you will not
ignore. (Psalm 51:17) (TLB)

For the LORD is good and his love endures forever;
his faithfulness continues through all generations.
(Psalm 100:5)

The name of the LORD is a fortified tower;
the righteous run to it and are safe. (Proverbs 18:10)

Trust in the LORD with all your heart
and lean not on your own understanding;
in all your ways submit to him,
and he will make your paths straight. (Proverbs 3:5–6)

He lets me rest in the meadow grass and leads me beside
the quiet streams. He gives me new strength. He helps
me do what honors him the most. (Psalm 23:2–3) (TLB)

PART 3

YOUR CHANGED HEART CHANGES EVERYTHING

CHAPTER 7

INSIDE OUT

A few years back, I was speaking to a group of youth workers at a local pizza parlor. I noticed a woman in the crowd who was distressed; she had tears in her eyes while constantly looking downward, folding her hands in front of her face as if she didn't want to make eye contact. After I spoke, she approached me and broke down, crying hysterically. She informed me that her problem was with her husband. She said he would stay out all night drinking night after night, and she didn't know when or if he would make it home. During our conversation, I told her that I just started a men's Bible study and asked her to invite him to attend or, if he were willing, I would speak with him myself.

The following week, to my surprise, her husband showed up to our men's Bible study. We will call him Bob. Bob was on crutches and seemed a bit disheartened as well. A few weeks later, Bob stayed after the other men went home; he wanted to talk and fill me in on his part of the circumstances. He stated that he worked at a local restaurant and was a social drinker. After a hard night's work, quite often, he would go out with other employees to drink and socialize. He often drank too much and would lose track of time, ending up in some bad predicaments, to the point that his wife had had enough, and she was ready to leave him.

Bob then told me how he broke his leg. "My wife was gone for the weekend at a women's retreat. So, after work on Friday night, I went out with the guys. I drank too much and woke up early in the morning in an open field, not knowing how I got there. I got up and started walking across the field to go home. I had to step over a barbed wire fence to get out of the field. As I was going over the fence, I slipped, and the barbed wire caught me under my leg, cut me up pretty bad, and shredded my slacks. As I continued walking past the fence, a short time later, I stepped the wrong way off the curb, and I fell and broke my leg. I had no choice but to keep going when I noticed an older man watching me from his living room window across the street. I was limping by his house, bleeding down my leg with shredded pants. I was wondering what the older man was thinking. I soon found out when the police showed up and arrested me!"

Bob attended the men's study regularly every week, and he appeared to have a real change of heart. I ran into his wife a couple of months later and asked how her husband was doing (if you want the truth, ask a man's wife!). She told me, "A short time ago, I was going to walk out the door, but he's a changed man; God must have gotten a hold of his heart. Now my only complaint is that he plays his Christian music too loudly in the house!"

I don't get it! I don't understand or comprehend it! How God does what He does in the heart and the life of a person. But one thing I do know based on my personal experience and numerous other testimonies is that He works from the inside out! Why is that so profound, you ask? You know if this message has taken root inside of you, for you feel a cleansing from guilt, pain, and shame that you have never known before. It's difficult to articulate because it is something that happens inside of you and often impacts each person individually. Considering our most imminent need of being loved and accepted mentioned in the previous chapter, to what lengths will we go to find the wisdom, love, joy, and peace to soothe and fulfill our human hearts?

My personal experience attempting to walk with God has revealed that upon our trust and submission to His divine providence in our lives, God takes residence on the inside. And as we continue to abide in His sovereign guidance, he proceeds to work from the inside out. That's right; God doesn't wait for us to clean up our acts or do better! He takes us just the way we are, with all our bad habits, preconceived notions, and hang-ups. I have found that what God has to offer me in my life is so much better than all the muck and mire from the past that I thought would bring some lasting satisfaction. Reflecting on Samaria is to understand God's heart for humanity. No person is too far out of His reach—no matter who you are or what you've done. Your ethnicity, culture, or gender makes no difference at all.

As human beings, we are divided in our love. God does not measure love. God can only love totally—100 percent all the time. If we think God is a person who can divide his love, then we are thinking not of God but ourselves. God is perfectly one, the perfect unity. We have love, but God is love. His love is not an activity. It is His whole essence.

LOVE IN ACTION

The Internet can be both a wonderful and awful resource, a vast array of different ideas and information. I couldn't help but scan the various blogs and articles that deal with this issue of finding fulfillment in life, again with a variety of answers. But the consensus is that we need to find our essential core values, inner wisdom, or evolved psychological state—that is, look within ourselves to find fulfillment, prioritizing our lives in finding what's important and making it happen!

All of this sounds fantastic—if it is obtainable, realistic, and lasting. I mean, what if my core values are not so constructive? What if I am not very wise, and my evolved state has progressed into more of a stalemate? Sometimes, looking within ourselves can have about the same value as walking or hanging out in a terrible neighborhood. I can't imagine that any of us can maintain our emotional and psychological stability in and of ourselves when the violent, turbulent storms of life wreak havoc in our lives. You know, the kind that flattens forests, collapses bridges, and demolishes homes, causing widespread damage and leaving a trail of destruction. But I do know a God that will sustain and even strengthen us through the most vicious and brutal storms that life can dish out.

I mentioned earlier that I had minimal to no previous Christian or any religious experience in my life before coming to know Jesus at the age of twenty-five. I thought that it was a good idea to have a Bible somewhere in your house, not that anybody could understand it! But God has a way of getting your attention even when you don't expect it.

After three years at California Correctional Institution, the institution where I had started my career in corrections, my wife Judy and I moved over to the central coast of California, where I ended my career at CMC California Men's Colony State Prison twenty-seven years later. I wanted to move for a couple of different reasons. First, to get away from my wife's meddling family, who always found a way to stay in our business; second, who doesn't want to live by the beach! I was anything but a model husband and father. I was selfish and irresponsible, wanting to party and run around, to do my thing with whom I wanted when I wanted.

My wife was a mess. She was a young mother with two young children, all by herself and separated from her family, her only support on whom she was reliant. She sure couldn't depend on me! She told me that she was going to start attending a small church that we had passed on occasion. I believe my response was, "Have a good time," or some other inconsiderate statement like that. During that same time, there seemed to be a problem in payroll at my previous prison. They failed to forward my monthly paycheck from the former prison where I was employed, and we were down to the bare necessities.

One Sunday afternoon, there was a knock at the front door, and I could see a couple of people standing outside with boxes in their hands. My wife answered the door, and these people proceeded into the living room, where I was perched up in my chair with a beer in my hand, watching a football game. One of the men walked up to me, where I was sitting and motioned to shake my hand. I was in the process of switching my beer from my right hand to the left when he introduced himself as the pastor of the church. He said that he knew a bit of our present situation and wanted to bring by a little money and groceries to help us out. Then he said, "Please don't feel uncomfortable or anything." I just knew that as I was holding a beer in my left hand and shaking this pastor's hand with my right, I was going to be struck by lightning, breathe my last, or something bad was going to happen! I wanted to become about three inches tall and disappear down in a crack of the chair somewhere. I laugh about it now, but at the time, I was anything but comfortable.

The following week, my wife asked me to attend a Halloween alternative party at the church with her. I figured that this type of event should be non-threatening enough to me, so I went along. I was amazed. There were young adults our age having a good time laughing and having fun. And they didn't seem to be in any way intoxicated. I found their behavior to be a bit profound.

The next step for me was attempting to go to church. I felt that if I went once, I could tell everyone that I was grateful for their generosity and feel better about myself, then disappear and never go back. So, although I was nervous and felt very uneasy, I decided to go to church one Sunday when another strange occurrence happened. The pastor's message was out of one of the New Testament epistles, and the context was referring to marriage and raising kids and other such rational things. Again, I was amazed. I always thought that the Bible was some out-of-date, ancient book that no one understood. I had no idea that it spoke of day-to-day practical things that were so applicable.

For me, it was a process over some time, but just the way I was with all my faults, doubts, and flagrant issues, God gripped my heart, and I have never been the same! No, I didn't say that I ever became perfect, and all my problems went away. I merely said that I have never been the same. In my life, there is no substitute for *His divine presence*!

When I came to the point of trusting Jesus at age twenty-five, I was astonished and utterly blindsided. I didn't see it coming, nor did I understand what just happened. But as I started to grow in this newfound relationship, I realized that God was changing me from the inside out. The process continues, and I still think of it as strange and bizarre!

For example, after a couple of years had gone by, I was having a conversation with a friend at work. We were talking about marriage and spending time with family. During our conversation, he looked at me with a sincere look on his face when he called me a "family man." I almost leaped out of my skin. It was somewhat frightening. Family man! What was that! I had no idea where he got that impression. I mentioned my dad passing when I was young and being brought up by a very unstable mother. I didn't think that I had any idea what it would take to be considered a family man. All these things started rushing through my mind when I realized that a transformation was taking place inside of me. My old desire was being removed, and God was filling me with a new desire.

I compare it with my old, scuba diving era. I used to do a lot of scuba diving all over the coast of California and down through Mexico. Besides spearfishing, another favorite target was abalone. During our dive, we would take our abalone bars and pop those tasty snails off the rocks. But that was only the beginning.

Preparation before consumption was a lot of work. You pried the abalone out of the shell, cut it into slices, and beat each slice with a rubber mallet repeatedly until you broke down the muscle. If you didn't complete this process, the ab meat is too tough, and it would be much like trying to chew on a piece of rubber. You don't just mix some ingredients, rub on some abalone steak tenderizer, and place it in the refrigerator. You are the tenderizer! But you see, in my case, God does the tenderizing from the inside. I don't think He uses a rubber mallet, but whatever He uses, apart from being frightening and sometimes painful, it sure has been effective in bringing about positive desire and change in my life. Again, not by any means "perfect," just not the same.

I had a terrible childhood. You could have hit me in the head with a shovel, and I wouldn't cry. I couldn't. I was too hard on the inside. Now my wife and kids make fun of me. I have been known to cry when certain music plays, during movies, and even watching television commercials! They don't even have to see my face when they comment in their sarcastic tone of voice, "Dad, do you need a tissue?" I have to wipe away the tears and gather myself together before saying, "You guys are really funny."

I could go on and on with my personal experiences and amazing stories from others, as to how God interceded, making a divine appointment, with His divine presence. But I would like to reference a real professional that I have been familiar with through the years. He is the late Dr. Gary Smalley, author of numerous books on family relationships, family counselor, and president and founder of Smalley Relationship Center. An article of his is at Crosswalk.com, titled "People, Places, and Things Are the Gifts of Life, Not the Source of Life."

From different painful experiences that I have been through, I've learned that I was looking for love, peace, and joy in all the wrong places. In other words, I had spent a lifetime looking for a sense of significance and security. However, I was looking for that in the wrong location. Since then, I've learned that we all have similar goals in life. If our lives were like a cup, each one of us would love to fill it with wisdom, love, joy, and peace. We'd like to have our lives overflow with positive emotions and genuine fulfillment in life. Unfortunately, most of us look to one of three sources, or all three, for the fullness of life we really want. Yet, like a mirage, these sources shimmer with fulfillment but only bring dust to our souls.

SOURCE #1
LOOKING TO PEOPLE TO FILL OUR CUPS

The first place many of us tend to look is to people. We think, *If I am to really have my needs met and be happy, I must have another person in my life.* However, those who look for people will ultimately find that they cannot fill our cups. Others can be frustrating and irritating and drain away as much emotional energy as they give—or more. Friends can be a tremendous source of help and encouragement at times, but even they can disappoint us over the long haul. We can look to friends as the source of positive emotions, but at times, they too can punch holes in our emotional lives.

SOURCE #2
LOOKING TO PLACES FOR FULFILLMENT

"We need a home! That's it; we need a place with a beautiful view and trees that are the envy of the neighborhood. If only we had the right place to live in, our cups would be full." How many of us have echoed these words? Or how about a vacation or a new office with a window? These certainly would fill our cups to the brim.

Then we buy that special home or go to that remote island, live in it for a short while, and suddenly our lives begin to go wrong. Why? In part because no matter how pretty or fulfilling places look, they don't fit inside our personal cups. Instead, they all have sharp edges that cut holes into our lives. What's more, the people we share them with are the people who drain our cups! But if people and places don't fill up the deepest part of our lives, where do we turn to finally find love, peace, and joy?

SOURCE #3
LOOKING TO THINGS FOR FULFILLMENT

How about more money so we can buy more things? Many of us feel that if we just had more money, we'd be happier in life. However, study after study of people who strike it rich shows this isn't the case. The more money we make, the more wisdom we must have to handle it. Now, I know many of us wouldn't mind learning that kind of wisdom, but to receive money, we normally have to pay a personal price. Money alone and all the things it can bring can't fill our lives with the kind of living water we desperately want. I've met people throughout the country who have little money and are miserable. I've also met those with lots of money who are miserable. I've known people who have mountain cabins and third cars who feel fulfilled. Some people I know barely have bus fare, and they feel fulfilled as well.

Most people who depend on "things" to fill up their cups end up looking for the one perfect job that will be the ticket to all their dreams. All jobs have work in common, and work doesn't always keep our cups full. It can drain us because of the people we work with, the place where we do our work, and the equipment we must use. Some of us try all our lives to acquire a key to a certain washroom in the company or parking spaces with our names on them. When we receive them, however, what do we have? Are we finally being filled with wisdom, love, peace, and joy? Hardly. Just the opposite is often true.

COMING UP EMPTY IN LIFE

At some times in our lives, we run headlong into an inescapable fact. Life is not fulfilling. It's actually often unfair and exhausting. By focusing on people, places, and things, we miss the positive emotions we want and are saddled with the negative emotions we've tried all our lives to avoid! This is true of hurt feelings, worry, anxiety, fear, unrest, uncertainty, and confusion because we are depending on a person, place, or thing for "life." We're all selfish in wanting others to cooperate in meeting our needs right now. But those who are wise realize there is a pathway to freedom, away from that unfulfilled feeling.

SEEKING FIRST THE SOURCE OF LIFE

Matthew 6:33 clearly shows us our Source of life: "But seek first His kingdom and His righteousness, and all these things will be given to you as well." In my life, when God is in first place, He promises to meet all my needs. He's the highest priority in my life. When I focus on Jesus Christ as the sole Source of my life, an amazing thing happens. Because He loves me and actually possesses the wisdom, love, peace, and joy I've always wanted, He alone can overflow my cup. That's exactly what He promises to do for His children: "This love…surpasses knowledge—that you may be filled to the measure of all the fullness of God." (Ephesians 3:19)

Can you be any more filled than full? Absolutely not. Psalm 62 says that we are to wait and hope in God alone. He's our rock, our salvation, our rearguard, our hiding place. He's everything we'll ever need! Nothing on this earth compares to knowing Him. (Philippians 3:7–9)

OUR HEIGHTENED SPIRITUAL AWARENESS

I believe it to be quite evident in our society that we have realized that there has to be something or someone that is a higher power, other than just ourselves. Whether that power is God or another source, the consensus being that man is not the highest power of the universe. Our struggle to trust and follow our guidance and direction to navigate life has become comical. In this crazy and mixed-up world, what makes sense anymore? With politics, religion, world finances, relationships, and media bias, we don't even know what or who to believe anymore. All of these are detrimental issues of life, and they make no lasting sense at all.

In all humanity, plenty of things don't make sense. If they are not important, that's reasonable. However, there are vital issues in life that should make sense (like the issues above), and don't, and that's not all right.

Why is a person who invests all your money called a broker?

Why did Japanese kamikaze pilots wear helmets?

Why call it quicksand if it takes you down slowly?

Why is there an expiration date on sour cream?

Why is it called a *pair* of pants?

Does it make any sense to fill in a form by filling it out?

Why call it Earth when it's 71 percent water?

Why are they called chicken fingers when chickens don't have fingers?

A life without God is like King Solomon put it so eloquently in the Book of Ecclesiastes, like "chasing after the wind." In this time of our heightened spiritual awareness—with all this madness going on all around us—we search for many substitutes for God. But there is none and never will be. God is in the life-transforming business. Only God, and God alone, understands the innermost being and desire of our hearts and minds.

It is an extraordinary thought to contemplate how God changes and transforms a person's life, a process that I surely don't understand because nobody can. That's what drives us so crazy. We would love to diagnose this process scientifically or psychologically to gain a full perception. God states that His way is so much higher than ours. I believe this is one of the ways that He makes that fact evident. But what we do have is the evidence of changed lives; my own life is one of them.

Having a relationship with God is not just an improvement. He goes with you wherever you go because He takes up residence on the inside. When God looks at you, He sees Jesus's righteousness, not your sin, and ultimate separation from Him. He will be your source of comfort. He is the Savior of the worst of sinners, hope in times of suffering, and your protector from digging up your same mess. He will become your very life. I have found that what does make perfect sense to me every day, all the time, is my intimate personal relationship with God, nothing else!

When you come to the point where you trust Him, you don't have to be a product of your parents or your past anymore, no longer a slave to your poor choices and bad decisions, ruled by your intellectual pride or those lies or bad experiences that have controlled you for so long. One choice will abolish all the others and bring you absolute freedom and make you right with our eternal judge and jury, and it will change your life now and determine your eternal destiny.

Again, not in any way am I telling you this to make you "religious." I am not trying to preach some make-believe fairy tale that will never come true. How do I know? Personal experience! It is the same choice that I was offered and received, and it changed my life forever. So just how and where does it all start?

Giving up doesn't always mean you're weak. Sometimes it just means you're strong enough to let go.

"God loves you more in a moment than anyone could in a lifetime." (thinke.org)

> You have searched me, LORD,
> and you know me.
> You know when I sit and when I rise;
> You perceive my thoughts from afar.
> You discern my going out and my lying down;
> You are familiar with all my ways.
> Before a word is on my tongue
> You, LORD, know it completely.
> You hem me in behind and before,
> and you lay your hand upon me.
> Such knowledge is too wonderful for me,
> too lofty for me to attain. (Psalm 139:1–6)

> Because of the LORD's great love, we are not consumed,
> for his compassions never fail.
> They are new every morning;
> great is your faithfulness. (Lamentations 3:22–23)

> And the peace of God, which transcends all understanding, will guard your hearts and your minds in Christ Jesus. (Philippians 4:7)

> I will give you a new heart and put a new spirit in you; I will remove from you your heart of stone and give you a heart of flesh. (Ezekiel 36:26)

The Spirit of the LORD GOD is upon me because the LORD has anointed me to bring good news to the suffering and afflicted. He has sent me to comfort the brokenhearted, to announce liberty to captives, and to open the eyes of the blind. (Isaiah 61:1) (TLB)

But whenever anyone turns to the Lord, the veil is taken away. (2 Corinthians 3:16)

Whoever does not love does not know God, because God is love. (1 John 4:8)

How priceless is your unfailing love, O GOD! People take refuge in the shadow of your wings. (Psalm 36:7)

Therefore, if anyone is in Christ, the new creation has come: The old has gone, the new is here! (2 Corinthians 5:17)

God is our refuge and strength,
an ever-present help in trouble. (Psalm 46:1)

The LORD is compassionate and gracious;
slow to anger, abounding in love. (Psalm 103:8)

He heals the brokenhearted
and binds up their wounds. (Psalm 147:3)

Let him have all your worries and cares, for he is always thinking about you and watching everything that concerns you. (1Peter 5:7) (TLB)

Love is patient, love is kind. It does not envy, it does not boast, it is not proud. It does not dishonor others, it is not self-seeking, it is not easily angered, it keeps no record of wrongs. Love does not delight in evil but rejoices with the truth. It always protects, always trusts, always hopes, always perseveres. (1 Corinthians 13:4–7)

God's love is amazing! First, John 4:16 says God is love. And verse 18 says, "There is no fear in love, but perfect love casts out fear …" God's love can remove fear from your life. It's a medicine that can heal every wound in your soul: a broken heart, the pain of rejection or abandonment, or any other hurt you've experienced.

– Joyce Meyer, author, and speaker

CHAPTER 8

JOURNEY TO THE WINNER'S CIRCLE

Ever notice that when someone passes away, all of a sudden, just about everyone has something good to say about them? They may have been awful, mean, and hateful, never having a nice thing to say about anybody, but when they pass, all of a sudden, they were a saint who never did anything wrong. I want to tell you about myself. I am not a hyper Bible-thumping religious person, but I am a realist. I want to convey the truth to you to the best of my ability just the way it is—no tricks or gimmicks. That is why I choose to incorporate so many of my personal stories and experiences.

You might have noticed that at no time throughout this book have I tried to convince you that God is real. God is real because He is real and alive in me every day. I have seen and personally witnessed Him transform and drastically change many lives, including my own, from lives riddled with hopelessness and despair to the individuals that seem to have it all together. Whether in prison, on the streets, with friends, relatives, or people that I have never met before, God is alive and well. He has proven Himself to me too many times to deny. In this chapter, I would like to share a few of those stories with you.

If you choose to disbelieve this fact and live in denial based on what you have been instructed, told after a bad experience, or for any other reason, I sure hope and pray that you reconsider. Please don't pass up the greatest gift ever offered humanity in history, not only in this life but also for the life to come.

GOD INTERVENES AND LIVES CHANGE

I was working as the yard sergeant in one of the quads at the prison early one Saturday morning before the breakfast meal release of the inmate population. The four separate yards on this facility each consist of two buildings with three floors. I was inside one of the buildings on the first-floor foyer, having a conversation with a couple of Christian correctional officers regarding their changed lives in Jesus and some other work-related issues. I had to end our conversation since I had to proceed to the dining hall to begin the breakfast meal release of the inmate population.

During our inmate population feeding process, I noticed a correctional officer, whom I had never met, toward the back of the dining room, supervising the seating. After an inmate has entered the dining hall and received his food tray, he is to sit at the next available seat regardless of who is already seated at his table and who he will sit beside. A correctional officer supervises this process in the dining room to ensure this procedure is followed. I walked over to his location to introduce myself.

Shortly into our dialogue, this officer—we will call him Officer Marcos—informed me that he was in the building on the third tier, listening to our earlier conversation before the meal release. He then asked me if I thought that if someone was in jail and claimed that they found Jesus and their life was changed, could it be real? His question caught me off guard; I was not expecting him to get so direct, being that we had just met and were in the dining hall with several inmates around making a lot of commotion.

I answered his question the best way I could, and then he informed me that he was inquiring about his wife. He said that she had been wrestling with a drug habit for years and had come to know Jesus in jail, claiming that her life was now changed forever. Marcos was having a hard time with the sincerity of her claim, so I asked him if he had a relationship with God. He immediately changed gears with a surprised look on his face, stating, "Oh no! I'm just asking about my wife!" I just had to laugh a bit, and I told him that I was just curious. We went on with our conversation.

A short time later, he asked me what I meant by having a relationship with God. I explained the simple, straightforward Gospel message to him and further told him that I had a Bible in my office downstairs if he would like to examine the Scripture for himself after feeding. Officer Marcos followed me to my office after the feeding procedure was over, and I showed him the Bible references that I was referring to earlier. I watched his facial expression change from peering and questioning to blissful and ecstatic within a matter of a few minutes as he examined the Scriptures.

At that time, it sure appeared to me that Marcos just had a serious encounter with God. So, I asked him if today was the day that he wanted to trust Jesus for the first time. He explained to me that he felt a bit odd committing to receive Christ in the prison while he was at work. So, I told him that it was entirely optional but that we could meet somewhere else at a later time if he desired.

At Marcos's request, we met on a small pier that overlooked the Back Bay waterfront. As we sat down on the pier and started our conservation, I noticed a small coffee shop located directly behind us, with a few outside tables and chairs on an open patio that was empty of any customers. There was nobody on the pier or anywhere around us. We started talking about a variety of different topics, such as family, raising children, and so forth. Our conversation eventually returned to where we had left off in at work, and he examined the Gospel message Scriptures once again. His whole disposition seemed to change again at that moment.

I again need to mention that at this time, there was still nobody on the small pier, anywhere around us, or at the coffee shop behind us.

The actual pier where the conversion took place.

Photo taken by my daughter Cassie Mooneyhan.

Officer Marcos then stated that it was his time to get right with God, so, we bowed our heads to pray. Only a few minutes in as we were finishing our prayer time together, we heard this beautiful worship music. We both turned around in the direction of the coffee shop and observed these two young women playing acoustic guitars and singing the most beautiful Christian music on the outside patio. We both looked at each other in amazement with tears in our eyes, and Officer Marcos stated, "Is that confirmation or what?"

On a warm summer day, while working as the watch sergeant, I had a conversation with a white supremacist inmate who had overheard me talking about spiritual issues with another individual. We will call him Jason. Jason was assigned as a watch office janitor in the building and had tattoos all over him: white pride on the back of both his arms, lightning bolts on his neck, along with a swastika and other identifying symbols. Jason approached me toward the back of the building and stated, "Sergeant, you don't actually believe any of that religious garbage that you were talking about earlier, do you?"

"Well, actually, I do. Why do you ask?"

"I was into that God thing when I was in the county jail. I was at an extremely low time in my life. Right after I was arrested, my girlfriend then left me, and I felt like my life was over. My cellmate in the county jail was a Christian and started telling me about Jesus and how Jesus changed his life and brought hope to his hopeless situation. After a couple of weeks, I got saved. I was speaking and ministering with quite a few of the county jail inmates about God, even opposing gang members, most of whom were Hispanic. Everything in my life changed and seemed so much better. Then God left me, so I forgot God and went about my own business!"

As Jason relayed to me how "God left him," he extended his middle finger in the air with the back of his hand toward me the obscene gesture of flipping someone off. I have to admit his statement and hand gesture upset me a bit, and I replied, "You bumped your head! That is so inconsistent, if not impossible, with God's character. We leave Him, but He never leaves us. What happened was you were getting too full of yourself, and God humbled you. It was necessary to remind you not to get too full of yourself and remember this ministry is not all about you. You turned and walked away, not God!"

Immediately after I made this statement, Jason's eyes rolled toward the back of his head, his knees buckled, and he grabbed on to a nearby wall, bracing himself so he wouldn't fall to the floor. Then my knees buckled slightly, and I leaned against the wall behind me. We both just stood there for a moment staring straight ahead in amazement and didn't speak a word. Jason then left abruptly to return to his dorm for the lunch meal release.

After lunch feeding was over, I noticed Jason had returned and was sweeping a floor in the back office. I approached and asked him what happened. He stated, "God just shook me up and rattled my cage. I didn't go to the chow hall and eat. I couldn't. I went back to my bed area and wrote my mom a letter, asking her to send me my Bible!"

Toward the end of Chapter Four, I briefly explained to you the workings of the lockup or administrative segregation unit. In this unit, we also housed GP, general population inmates, along with different classifications of inmates in the Mental Health Services Delivery System.

During the time our segregation staff and I would be processing inmate showers on the tier, we would talk about a variety of subjects, from sports to politics, and also on occasion, spiritual issues. There were a couple of other staff members on the tier who were also Christian, so we would speak openly about what God was doing in our lives. As I was walking down the tier toward the office just after we had finished showering the inmates on the tier one morning, an inmate yelled, "Sergeant!" from his cell window as I was walking by. We will call him Martin.

I approached Martin's cell window to find out why he was trying to get my attention. Martin was a flamboyant gay black male inmate. He was sitting on the floor in the back of his cell, and he seemed to be very agitated. He then informed me that he heard some of the other staff members and me talking about church and Jesus and that "it was all a bunch of nonsense." Then he told his story: "When I was younger and straight, I went to church all the time. I was raised in a Christian home with Christian parents—and look how I turned out! It's all a bunch of nonsense!"

I explained to Martin that we all have choices to make in life, some good and some maybe not so good—that at some time, he chose to become the person that he is today and that he has no reason to sit back and blame God for his personal choices. I told him that just as he chose to become who he is, he could also decide to change, but either way, God would love and accept him just the way he was! After our conversation had gone on for a while, Martin seemed to calm down a bit when he asked me to bring him a Bible, and I did.

A short time later, I received a job change and was reassigned to the culinary sergeant position in the central part of the prison, where all the food for the inmate population was prepared. To be quite honest, after a while, I had forgotten my conversation with inmate Martin in the administrative segregation unit—or I just wasn't much thinking about it.

One morning, I was walking across the second-floor kitchen area when an inmate approached and asked to speak with me. I said sure, and he said, "Sergeant, you probably don't remember me, but my name is inmate Martin. You and I had a conversation on the Ad Seg Tier, and you brought me a Bible to my cell. I just needed to tell you that I am back walking with Jesus. I hold a Bible study on the yard with mostly gay inmates. They are coming to know the Lord all the time, and it's so exciting! Sergeant, I am about to start crying. You know I can't stand here and cry in front of you in prison, so I have to go now. Thank you!" And he walked away.

After, I stood there, stunned for a couple of minutes. I just had to proceed to an outside viewing area, take in some fresh air, and reflect on what a great and wonderful God we serve!

In my life, I have experienced numerous other encounters like the three that I just described to you. I am not even going to try to convince you that it was God who intervened during the accounts that I just mentioned; you will have to decide that for yourself. However, I know beyond a shadow of a doubt what took place. I was personally involved in every occurrence and so many others. I was astonished and dumbfounded then and am still as I recall and write about it today. It serves to burn a hole in my soul where I could never forget or deny God's divine providence in the life of a human being.

The point is that there is no way for us to dissect or scientifically examine God's involvement or participation in the life of a human being. The fact that we cannot scientifically comprehend an infinite God often leads to frustration, doubt, and, many times, disbelief. We feel as if we have to fully understand and analyze God and "all His ways," put Him under a microscope, so to speak. But this is not what God is asking us to do. Because His ways are so much higher than ours, this task would be impossible.

I don't want to serve a God that I can fully understand and comprehend. If I could put God in a box or completely understand everything about Him, then He is not God at all; He's just another theory or experiment. God chooses to explain so many more tangible things that relate to us, such as His divine love for humanity, His perfect plan of redemption, and He allows us to partake in a beautiful existence in this life and the next, full of purpose and truth.

FINDING OUR WAY THROUGH THE DARKNESS

If God's tangible providential intentions are true, then why is there so much separation? In other words, why are we not better connected with God? We have numerous people moving in multiple directions—our social and cultural diversity, generational differences, intellectual, rich, and poor, and so on. Most seem to be moving in different directions with dissimilar interests and entirely different intentions.

There is always going to be the underlying factor that we are going to be insistent on doing it our way, what we are comfortable with, or what seems right to us.

Putting all that aside, I will do my best to explain solid biblical teaching that I believe is the biggest stumbling block for all of humanity. It determines where I start and how I can conduct and carry out all of my counseling procedures. I believe it will shed some light on our way through the darkness and explain this misconnection that we as people have toward God and where it derives from, causing unnecessary diversity and separation.

Just in case you didn't know, the misconnection that I am about to share with you is entirely spiritual. The idea that man is a triune being with a threefold nature—body, soul, and spirit—is something we need to understand about our identity as human beings. This reality was exposed in Chapter four but is explained in more detail below. Here is a partial blog post from Mark Henderson, founder of *The Inspired Legacy*, dated January 21, 2018, titled "3 Parts of a Complete Man."

> So, what is a *complete man*? To understand this, we must first understand what makes a man, or any human, for that matter. In simple terms, people are *spirits* who have a *soul* and live in a *body*.

We are a three-part whole divinely created to be God-conscious, self-conscious, and world-conscious. However, to operate in a manner consistent with our divine creation, we need to understand the function of each part.

Body

The body, sometimes referred to as our "flesh," is purely physical and consists of our five senses: hearing, smell, sight, touch, and taste. It's our physical shell that the world sees but is only temporary in terms of eternity.

Soul

The soul is who we are as individuals. It's where our emotions, reason, will, desire, and personality comes from. Our choices, feelings, and self-image all come from our soul. It's the window between our body and our spirit.

Spirit

The spirit is eternal, and if you're a believer in Christ, it's where he resides in you. Our faith, hope, and love come from our spirit. It's the source of our inner light.

Although it is conveyed several places throughout the Bible, the portion of Scripture that I want to use to make my point is located in the New Testament book of Ephesians Chapter 2, verses 1 through 10. The context is the Apostle Paul writing to Christians in a church called Ephesus, in what was then called Asia Minor (modern-day Turkey). In this passage of Scripture, Paul makes it clear that we are born **physically** alive but **spiritually** dead, his reference to the

Ephesian believers being once "dead in their transgressions and sins," but also through Christ how they were "made alive."

They were physically alive during the time Paul was writing to them; therefore, Paul is addressing how they became alive spiritually. Three other points of interest in the following Scripture are that Paul points out three critical changes that took place in these Ephesian believers once they put their faith in Christ: they have a position in heaven, they had nothing to do with it, and God now has a plan and purpose for their lives.

MADE ALIVE IN CHRIST

As for you, you were dead in your transgressions and sins, in which you used to live when you followed the ways of this world and of the ruler of the kingdom of the air, the spirit who is now at work in those who are disobedient. All of us also lived among them at one time, gratifying the cravings of our flesh and following its desires and thoughts. Like the rest, we were by nature deserving of wrath. But because of his great love for us, God, who is rich in mercy, made us alive with Christ even when we were dead in transgressions—it is by grace you have been saved. And God raised us up with Christ and seated us with him in the heavenly realms in Christ Jesus, in order that in the coming ages he might show the incomparable riches of his grace, expressed in his kindness to us in Christ Jesus. For it is by grace you have been saved, through faith—and this is not from yourselves, it is the gift of God—not by works, so that no one can boast. For we are God's handiwork, created in Christ Jesus to do good works, which God prepared in advance for us to do. (Ephesians 2)

I have mentioned before and will reiterate now that I am not and never will be a Bible-thumper or right-wing fanatic, just a couple of the crazy titles that I have heard through the years! But I do pride myself in being a realist, being that I like to view things as they are. All is not lost, but we do have a huge gaping hole in our society that causes division and separation rather than unity. With a few rare exceptions, most would say that there is nothing like getting together and spending time with family. I think it's clearly pointed out in the Scripture text that God intended us as a civilization to be one big family, dysfunctional at times, of course, but a family, nonetheless. We could point our fingers at all that's wrong in our world today and continue to be frustrated; however, we do need to realize that real and lasting positive change first starts with you and me as individuals.

If you have been reading this book from cover to cover, then you have discovered that God is not looking for you to have all the answers; you don't and never will this side of heaven. But I do hope that you have fully discovered two things about yourself as you took your journey on your road through Samaria: that you are not necessarily who you thought you were, and that God can and is willing to make a divine change in you from the inside out.

So now I hope you will consider not only thinking with your head, where you think you need to have all the answers—but begin to start thinking with your heart, where we learn to trust.

I want to show you a biblical example of a life that transitioned from "spiritual death" to "spiritual life," where Jesus clearly describes this process.

JESUS TEACHES NICODEMUS

Now there was a Pharisee, a man named Nicodemus who was a member of the Jewish ruling council. He came to Jesus at night and said, "Rabbi, we know that you are a teacher who has come from God. For no one could perform the signs you are doing if God were not with him."

Jesus replied, "Very truly I tell you, no one can see the kingdom of God unless they are born again."

"How can someone be born when they are old?" Nicodemus asked. "Surely they cannot enter a second time into their mother's womb to be born!"

Jesus answered, "Very truly I tell you, no one can enter the kingdom of God unless they are born of water and the Spirit. Flesh gives birth to flesh, but the Spirit gives birth to spirit. You should not be surprised at my saying, 'You must be born again.' The wind blows wherever it pleases. You hear its sound, but you cannot tell where it comes from or where it is going. So it is with everyone born of the Spirit."

"How can this be?" Nicodemus asked.

"You are Israel's teacher," said Jesus, "and do you not understand these things? Very truly I tell you, we speak of what we know, and we testify to what we have seen, but still you people do not accept our testimony. I have spoken to you of earthly things and you do not believe; how then will you believe if I speak of heavenly things? No one has ever gone into heaven except the one who came from heaven—the Son of Man. Just as Moses lifted up the snake in the wilderness, so the Son of Man must be lifted up, that everyone who believes may have eternal life in him."

For God so loved the world that he gave his one and only Son, that whoever believes in him shall not perish but have eternal life. For God did not send his Son into the world to condemn the world, but to save the world through him. Whoever believes in him is not condemned, but whoever does not believe stands condemned already because they have not believed in the name of God's one and only Son. This is the verdict: Light has come into the world, but people loved darkness instead of light because their deeds were evil. Everyone who does evil hates the light and will not come into the light for fear that their deeds will be exposed. But whoever lives by the truth comes into the light, so that it may be seen plainly that what they have done has been done in the sight of God. (John 3)

May God himself, the God of peace, sanctify you through and through. May your whole spirit, soul and body be kept blameless at the coming of our Lord Jesus Christ. The one who calls you is faithful, and he will do it.
(1 Thessalonians 5:23–24)

The human spirit is the lamp of the LORD that sheds light on one's inmost being. (Proverbs 20:27)

My shield is GOD Most High, who saves the upright in heart. (Psalm 7:10)

My flesh and my heart may fail, but GOD is the strength of my heart and my portion forever. (Psalm 73:26)

Teach me your way, LORD, that I may rely on your faithfulness; give me an undivided heart, that I may fear your name. (Psalm 86:11)

Teach us to number our days that we may gain a heart of wisdom. (Psalm 90:12)

Search me, GOD, and know my heart; test me and know my anxious thoughts. (Psalm 139:23)

Let love and faithfulness never leave you; bind them around your neck, write them on the tablet of your heart. (Proverbs 3:3)

Before ruin a person's heart is proud, but humility comes before honor.
(Proverbs 18:12) Tree of Life Version (TLV)

But if I say, "I will not mention his word or speak any more in his name," his word is in my heart like a fire, a fire shut up in my bones. I am weary of holding it in; indeed, I cannot. (Jeremiah 20:9)

You will seek me and find me when you seek me with all your heart. (Jeremiah 29:13)

I will give them an undivided heart and put a new spirit in them; I will remove from them their heart of stone and give them a heart of flesh. (Ezekiel 11:19)

For where your treasure is, there your heart will be also. (Matthew 6:21)

God, who knows the heart, showed that he accepted them by giving the Holy Spirit to them, just as he did to us. (Acts 15:8)

For this people's heart has become calloused; they hardly hear with their ears, and they have closed their eyes. Otherwise, they might see with their eyes, hear with their ears, understand with their hearts and turn, and I would heal them. (Acts 28:27)

And the peace of God, which transcends all understanding, will guard your hearts and your minds in Christ Jesus. (Philippians 4:7)

Let the peace of Christ rule in your hearts, since as members of one body you were called to peace. And be thankful. (Colossians 3:15)

May the Lord direct your hearts into God's love and Christ's perseverance. (2 Thessalonians 3:5)

CHAPTER 9

MAKING SENSE
OF IT ALL

think it's sad and comical, but don't we human beings eventually corrupt just about everything that we control or get our hands-on? I once had an inmate in the prison system tell me why our judicial system is so damaged. He said that judges are ex-attorneys and most—not all, but a vast majority of—attorneys are crooks; *you've all heard the jokes*! So, we have criminals running our judicial system, and we sit back and wonder why it's such a mess!

Through the years, I have heard numerous stories about people who have been hurt, derailed, or just downright lied to about who God is and how He intervenes into our hearts and lives. I love hearing people's stories, whether good, bad, or indifferent. I can tell you with absolute assurance regarding religious establishments or organizations that none are in any way exempt from the possibility of corruption or fraudulence.

Based on numerous testimonials and my personal experience, this area seems to cause a real stumbling block as to how many people view the church and ultimately God Himself. You normally don't go to some local lodge or country club and share your innermost personal thoughts and feelings. But the chances are that if you jump into a church with both feet and get involved with all the activities, eventually you will share delicate matters going on in your life, which could potentially put you in a vulnerable position.

I have had my feelings crushed, and my family temporarily adversely affected by the infrastructure and politics within the church. Although at the time the incidents that took place seemed completely overwhelming, as I trusted God further to see me through this difficult time, I eventually realized that through it all, I was being educated and strengthened. Yes, I had those overwhelming thoughts of just giving up, throwing in the towel, and saying, "I'm out of here!" But I realized that although God didn't cause the pain, He was using the pain to change me in different ways, and I have to admit that I have always felt so much closer to God when going through my suffering. Although it's never been pleasant, He meets me right where I am. He is always making necessary preparations in my life that will help me see and understand situations and circumstances from His perception and not my own. Looking back, I see that because God was involved, my suffering has never been meaningless or in vain; it has served to expand my capacity for compassion and gratitude.

When we travel down the road of suffering, although not pleasant at the time, we stand to learn many lessons that make our lives better and stronger in the end if God is involved. Every congregation consists of a bunch of imperfect people trying to serve a perfect God; nobody has "arrived," for we are all a work in progress. Those two facts alone are enough to cause major issues of turmoil, even with the best and most sincere intentions.

With all that said, whether warranted or not, there are some wounded and dejected people due to their encounters with those who would attempt to misguide and manipulate, whether parents, pastors, congregations, and a host of different entities representing religion, but this I can assure you: Jesus never did you that way! Religion or those who are representing religion, quite possibly, but not Jesus! I am not trying to discredit or deny the negative experience that you may have encountered. I know it happens; I have had a couple of episodes of my own! The reason that I mention this is that in my experience, so many somehow choose to turn away and to blame God.

It stands to reason that through some of these adverse circumstances, whether legit or not, it would breed many long-standing misconceptions about the church, who God is, and what having a personal relationship with Him is like. I can say with absolute certainty that most people know certain things about God but also know very little about the God of the Bible.

This portion of an article written by Wesley Baines from Belief. net will shed some light on our subject.

> Christianity is the largest religion on the planet in terms of believers. It's also one of the most misunderstood—even by its own adherents.
>
> The truth is that Christianity has changed a lot since Jesus walked the earth, and not all of that change has been positive. Between people and God have come obscuring layers of tradition, misinformation, ignorance, and wishful thinking, making it difficult for anyone—believers and nonbelievers alike—to find out who God is anymore.
>
> This is a huge problem. Christianity purports to teach believers how to live a moral life, and how to go about making our world the best place it can be. When we misunderstand the character of God, both missions can become seriously warped.
>
> And with Christianity having 2.2 billion adherents, this warped view stands to do some serious damage— when you don't truly know what Scripture says about God, you can justify just about anything in the name of Christianity.

Regardless of *where* or from *whom* we have derived our theology, it is evident that a lot of misleading propaganda from different sources has been circulated. Therefore, I would like to address a few of these misunderstandings to help us potentially establish an initial, or even reestablish an existing relationship of trust.

WHERE CAN WE PUT OUR TRUST?

> *Hypocrites: "I won't go to church; there are too many hypocrites!"*

Hypocrisy is the contrivance of a false appearance of virtue or goodness, while concealing real character or inclinations, especially with respect to religious and moral beliefs; hence, in a general sense, hypocrisy may involve dissimulation, pretense, or a sham. (Wikipedia)

Through the years, I have heard this statement affirmed more than any other, so we will start here with hypocrisy in the church. I am not about to deny that hypocrisy is present in the church. But hypocrisy is present everywhere in our culture: politics, media, Hollywood. Everyone is suspicious of everybody else, and we don't know who to trust, because deception is everywhere. We like to make people believe that we are better than we are.

Based on what you have heard or been told, it is extremely weak and easy to stand on the outside the church and throw rocks with your biased opinions and preconceived notions. Do some things need to change? Well, get involved and develop a relationship with the local parishioners and the church board. Let them hear your ideas, outlook, and viewpoints. There is no perfect church; I like to tease people and tell them that if they do find a perfect church, then don't join because it then just became imperfect. Because it sure would be if I joined it! But if it's a healthy church with even reasonably sincere people, then they will welcome your input and ideas, maybe also give you some information from a different perspective that you never thought about or considered!

If you discern that you are just spinning your wheels and getting nowhere, then it might be a good idea to move on to somewhere else. You will find that it won't take long until God sets up that divine appointment, and you find out where you need to be. But don't just sit home and blame God. God is perfect, and we are not. We are a work in progress, and we imperfect humans cause all the problems and make a mess of things. Yes, there are hypocrites in the church, but where else should they be? No one leaves a gym if they see an overweight person there. Where else should they be? The gym's purpose is to help people improve their condition.

No one gets upset going to a hospital and states they will never step foot in it again because there are too many sick people. Again, where else should they be? Nobody is perfect, and people will make mistakes, but God can forgive, cleanse, and restore. Also, we cannot always assume that everyone who is in the church has the church in them or is even there for the right reason. Therefore, we are to help them grow and mature. God will deal with it; He is the only one qualified to do so.

Jesus called out hypocrisy in a lot of people, but especially the religious leaders. Some Christians act hypocritically. What about all those who do not? What about all those who consistently live out the love of Christ in the world? In my experience, the vast majority of Christians are genuine, and a very small minority are hypocrites, still, we tend to focus and point out the minority when it is to our advantage.

A quote by Josh McDowell, apologist, evangelist, former agnostic, author or co-author of more than 150 books:

> "Christianity does not stand or fall on the way Christians have acted throughout history or are acting today. Christianity stands or falls on the person of Jesus, and Jesus was not a hypocrite. He lived consistently what He taught. Since Christianity depends on Jesus, it is incorrect to try to invalidate the Christian faith by pointing to horrible things done in the name of Christianity."

BIBLE OUT OF DATE: CONTRADICTIONS

The Bible is out of date, and there are all kinds of contradictions!

When it comes to documents that make up the Bible, we do not have the original manuscripts. Plus, there are variants in the copies that survived. Most are minor, but there you have it. We are faced with the question: without originals, can we still trust the Bible? Here are a few facts about the Bible to consider.

According to Wikipedia, the New Testament has been preserved in more manuscripts than any other ancient works of literature. In the New Testament alone, we have 10,000 Latin, 5,800 complete or fragmented Greek, and 9,300 manuscripts in various other ancient texts, all from which we compile and verify the accuracy of the Bible, which is thousands more than Homer's or Aristotle's works.

All of these manuscripts, fragments, scrolls, and parchments have been checked and double-checked for mismatches (known as variants), and most are a letter turned around or minor things that do not change the meaning of the story at all. The original writings were written on animal skins and other materials that deteriorated rapidly. What we have are copies of copies of the originals.

The value of having a large number of manuscripts is that it provides us with ample opportunity to compare writings, which is especially valuable when cross-checking manuscripts from different geographic areas or from different time periods.

Between 1947 and 1956, the Dead Sea Scrolls were discovered. Fragments of almost every book of the Old Testament were found, dating only two hundred years after the last Old Testament event took place.

The scribes who copied and recopied these documents were so incredibly careful that there is only about a 10 percent difference from the bits we have from 800 BC compared to the copies we have from AD 1500. It is almost impossible to imagine how they could have been so precise. Because of the great reverence, the Jewish scribes held toward the Scriptures; they exercised extreme care in making new copies of the Hebrew Bible. The entire scribal process was specified in meticulous detail to minimize the possibility of even the slightest error. The number of letters, words, and lines were counted, and the middle letters of the Pentateuch and the Old Testament were determined. If a single mistake were discovered during the examination of the manuscript, the entire manuscript would be destroyed. Putting together all of the manuscripts and comparing them with the Bible we have today, it is estimated that we have 99.5 percent of what would be considered the original document.

The Bible was written under the inspiration of the Holy Spirit by over forty different authors from all lifestyles: shepherds, farmers, tentmakers, physicians, anglers, priests, philosophers, and kings on three different continents, under an array of different circumstances, the heights of joy, and the depth of sorrow. Despite these differences in occupation, circumstances, geographical settings, and the span of approximately 1,600 years it took to write it, the Bible is an extremely cohesive and unified book. From the first book of the Bible, Genesis, where paradise is lost, to the last book of the Bible, Revelation, where paradise is gained, the Bible is one continuing story, the redemption of humanity.

The Holy Bible has been translated into 2,018 languages, with countless more partial translations and audio translations (for unwritten languages). Over two thousand is an enormous amount of translations. In comparison, Shakespeare, considered by many to be the master writer of the English language, has only been translated into fifty languages.

There are so many more truths regarding the validity and legitimacy of the Bible; however, the Bible has been the most persecuted book in history by far, for many different reasons, but I believe one major reason is that of translation.

> Translation: the rendering of something written or spoken in one language in words of a different language.

This is the *Encarta Dictionary* definition of translation. We can tell by definition alone that the possibility of a slight issue of divergence could erupt, "rendering one language to another."

The Bible was written in three different languages: Hebrew, Greek, and parts in Aramaic. There are generally three different categories of Bible translation consisting of word-for-word or literal, thought-for-thought, or paraphrase.

The Bibles that most closely follow the copies of the original manuscripts are word-for-word translations and essentially literal translations, the latter meaning they give the most accurate presentation of the original manuscripts.

Thought-for-thought translations move away from a word-for-word or literal approach and aim to transfer the meaning of phrases or groups of words from the original to an English equivalent.

Paraphrased translations help to make the Bible easier to read and understand for some people than the word-for-word or thought-for-thought translations.

With all this in mind, any time you attempt to translate Hebrew, Greek, or Aramaic into any other dialect—English, Spanish, French, Chinese, or any other language—there is bound to be translation error involved. No two languages are identical. However, these errors are minuscule in nature and do not affect the big picture or any of the vital context of the Bible message.

In this divine relationship, we get to know who God is, His will for our lives, and so many other amazing and life-changing things by reading the Bible. I love the Scripture in Hebrews 4:12, where the Bible is described as alive and active in our lives, penetrating soul and spirit, judging the thoughts and intents of the heart.

But keep in mind that God doesn't ask us for utter devotion to a written word. He asks us for utter devotion to the *God* of that written word!

There are multiple online resources available for further research into the overwhelming evidence to authenticate the Bible in crucial areas such as the following:

- Archaeology: Dr. Nelson Glueck, by consensus the greatest modern authority on Israeli archaeology, said, "No archeological discovery has ever controverted a biblical reference. Archeology continues to confirm a clear outline or in exact detail historical statements in the Bible."
- Prophecy: No other book on the planet can match the Bible's accuracy in foretelling events, for 30 percent of the Bible consists of prophecy, and not one of its prophecies has ever been inaccurate or shown to be false.

The Bible has stood the test of time under constant opposition and remains the best-selling book of all time and is very capable of bringing about personal, spiritual, and eternal change in one's life.

MY GOOD WORKS

God will accept me because I am a good person, obey the law, do not hurt anybody, help people in need, and so on.

I remember a story a pastor told me about the time he was starting his position as lead pastor in a church located in a bad neighborhood in Florida. He said that right after he and some congregants would paint over the gang graffiti on the side of the church, it would show up again within just a matter of days. The pastor was fed up dealing with this issue.

One night he was outside and noticed a group of gang members hanging out in the park located across the street from the church. So, he approached the guys in the park and explained his frustration with the recurring graffiti on the church walls. The fellas told him that they were quite sure they knew who was doing it—that they would watch out for the church and see to it that it wouldn't happen again. The pastor went on to tell me that the entire time he was pastoring the church, they never again had a problem with graffiti!

I use this story as an example. I don't think the fellas felt that their deed of watching over the church would get them to heaven. I lean more toward their feeling it was a gallant mission of respect, although some would choose to believe that their good works or deeds this side of heaven will somehow be enough to tip God's scale in their favor and earn them a place in heaven. I want to use part of an article I found on truelife.org to help us gain a better understanding of God's standard to answer this question.

If you believe being a good person is enough to get you into heaven, you're not alone. A variety of religions teach that people will be rewarded after death if they simply do more good deeds than bad ones. But this is not what the Bible teaches. Also, this kind of thinking often leaves us with more questions than answers.

For example, what exactly is the definition of a good person? Is a good person just anyone who doesn't commit a serious crime? Or maybe the bar is higher? Maybe being good also means working at a food kitchen once per week, serving the less fortunate. Or maybe it should be twice per week. How do we know how high the bar is set—and how can we know if we made the cut?

Others say that you simply need to do just enough good deeds to tip the scales. If all your good deeds make up at least 51 percent of what you do, then heaven should be your final destination. But how can you be sure that at least a little more than half of your life has been good? And don't some good and bad deeds carry more weight than others? The answers to all these questions will vary depending on who you talk to.

The Bible, however, clearly teaches that even our best attempts at being good fall short of God's high standard.

Romans 3:12 says, "There is no one who does what is good." Romans 3:23 says that all have "sinned and fallen short of the glory of God." In short, even the best person among us falls far short of what God expects. His standard is complete perfection and obedience; no one has ever met that standard except Jesus.

You may be thinking to yourself, Wait a minute! That seems a little extreme. I've done so many good things and kept almost all of the commandments in the Bible! I've never hurt anyone. I'm not perfect, but I'm certainly better than most people I know.

But James 2:10 says, "For the person who keeps all of the laws except one is as guilty as a person who has broken all of God's laws." Just one act of disobedience in an otherwise good life is all it takes to be found guilty and worthy of punishment in the eyes of God.

Think about it this way. Imagine that you're an accountant for a multimillion-dollar corporation. You're a good person who works hard and takes care of your family. But one day all that money becomes too tempting and you embezzle several thousand dollars. Will a judge let you off the hook for embezzlement just because you didn't murder anyone or deal drugs to children? No. You may have kept all the other laws of the land, but you're still a lawbreaker, and breaking the law has consequences.

You may be wondering at this point what hope anyone has of going to heaven if what the Bible says is true. That's a great question! The answer is that no one has any hope of escaping God's judgment, apart from trusting in Jesus.

What does that mean? It means that God's forgiveness depends on faith or trust in Jesus, not works. It can't be earned by us. Jesus alone earned it for us. Nobody deserves it. Nobody can work for it. It is a gracious gift from God.

God was not going to make an exception for you or anyone else. Sin had to be atoned for; our wrongs had to be made right in God's eyes. That's why only Jesus can pay the penalty for our sins. There is no substitute for what only God can do.

I'M NOT GOOD ENOUGH

God cannot save or use me; I have gone too far!

It seems at one time or another we have all been misinformed or led to believe a huge lie! The only way that we will ever measure up is to be perfect, blameless, and conform to our version of how to be a believer or Christian. This message can generate from a variety of different people or places: parents, church, parishioners, school, society, and the list goes on. "If you were a real Christian, you wouldn't say that, act that way, or have those thoughts!" I like to think that when people are pointing one finger at me, there are three more pointing back at them, and the most important finger, the thumb, is pointing upward!

According to the American Medical Association's "Guides to the Evaluation of Permanent Impairment," your thumb is so important that a complete amputation "will result in a 40 percent impairment to the whole hand." In fact, they claim that it would take "a complete amputation of the middle, ring, and small fingers to equal the impairment of an amputated thumb."

I want to assure you that there is nowhere in the Bible that any human being is referred to as perfect. The Bible is very transparent in revealing the flaws of all the great heroes of the faith. We are encouraged to have perfect intentions and strive toward perfection, which describes the process of spiritual development. But the purpose of this process is union with God, characterized by a pure love of God and other people, with the ultimate goal of spiritual maturity. But to be "perfect," no.

Many destructive behaviors can surface in our lives from the unattainable goal of perfectionism if taken too seriously. According to Healthline, – People with perfectionism hold themselves to impossibly high standards. They think what they do is never good enough. Perfectionism can lead to depression, anxiety, eating disorders, and a host of other self-destructive behaviors. Even mild cases can interfere with your quality of life.

Whether we are feeling deadened by the thoughts of our seemingly hopeless present or being bombarded by the muck and mire of our pasts, we can somehow reach a point of no return where we know that our lives as we know them are over, no chance that God can or will use us. Allow me to use a highly philosophical word here: *hogwash*. God can and will use anybody, especially the underdog!

Gideon thought very little of himself, but God didn't. The Midianites, Amalekites, and other Eastern people used to take his lunch money, so to speak—more like his and his people's crops. They were severely oppressed by the neighboring peoples, who were much stronger, taking their food supply and other necessities. God called Gideon and referred to him as a "mighty warrior." Gideon's response: "Pardon me, my Lord, but how can I save Israel? My clan is the weakest in Manasseh, and I am the least in my family." Despite Gideon's lack of self-confidence, God used him mightily and brought about a great victory.

Deborah was a prophet and leader of Israel. Her people, the Israelites, were cruelly oppressed by the Canaanites. Barak, the military general in charge of Israel's army, wouldn't even go to battle without Deborah being with him. Deborah led Israel during a time in history where men dominated leadership positions, but that didn't stop her from being a powerful influence and a great mediator, advisor, counselor, and leader. God delivered Sisera and the entire Canaanite army into her hands.

God could have used the rich and famous, the strong and popular. Instead, He used twelve disciples from some of the lowest places and backgrounds on earth to change the entire world forever! God chooses leaders by His standards, not ours.

RELIGION IS FOR THE WEAK

Religion is for the weak is another false statement sometimes accepted as truth. You are too weak to deal with life and make it on your own. So, you have to get religion to use as a crutch, to stand on your own two feet and make it through life.

I previously mentioned working in the segregation lockup unit at the prison, during which time we had many crazy, violent, and absurd issues erupt; cutters, hangers, fights on the exercise yard and in the showers, and cell extractions, to name a few. All of our daily work activities and issues served to build quite a strong camaraderie among our staff since we were working together in tight quarters. I was never a Bible-thumper in any way, but I was upfront about my relationship with God.

While on the tier or in the office, we would talk about a wide range of subjects, and of course, there was the normal cutting up, being sarcastic, and making fun of each other. While we would engage in conversations, most of my comrades would use foul language. However, in the rare incident that I happened to slip up and say anything even remotely improper, all eyes were on me. There were comments like, "Did you hear what the sergeant said?" They would make a big deal about it for a long time. The other guys could use foul language multiple times every day and nobody cared, but for me, it was altogether different! It was as if my life and actions were under a microscope, and I was accountable. Don't get me wrong; my coworkers would laugh and make a big joke about it, but they were sure to point it out and make fun of me, nonetheless.

Being held more accountable is just one of the ways that my life is much more trying in Christ. But I can assure you that God's providence and blessing in my life far outweigh any tribulation. I would not trade back who I am in Christ for anything! My life has never been more difficult in certain areas than after trusting Christ. Such as in the above example of being held accountable for my actions verbally. My relationship with God is a great strength physically, mentally, and spiritually and has never been a weakness or some type of crutch that I need to help me contend with life.

There are many more examples that I could give you regarding this subject. However, the Bible makes it very clear that we are all flawed, scared, and imperfect, and that's exactly why we need the Savior. So please understand that we are all in the same position and condition together. You belong, your life matters, and God loves you just the way you are! We didn't find God. God found us. We don't make ourselves holy through certain practices. God's perfect love calls to us, and if we respond to His call with a willing heart, He will plant the seed of perfect love in our hearts, and we'll go forward from there.

Here are a couple of examples from the book of Matthew of Jesus calling out the religious leaders as hypocrites.

PAYING THE IMPERIAL TAX TO CAESAR

Then the Pharisees went out and laid plans to trap him in his words. They sent their disciples to him along with the Herodians. "Teacher," they said, "we know that you are a man of integrity and that you teach the way of God in accordance with the truth. You aren't swayed by others, because you pay no attention to who they are. [17] Tell us then, what is your opinion? Is it right to pay the imperial tax to Caesar or not?"

But Jesus, knowing their evil intent, said, "You hypocrites, why are you trying to trap me? [19] Show me the coin used for paying the tax." They brought him a denarius, [20] and he asked them, "Whose image is this? And whose inscription?"

"Caesar's," they replied.

Then he said to them, "So give back to Caesar what is Caesar's, and to God what is God's."

When they heard this, they were amazed. So, they left him and went away. (Matthew 22:15–22)

SEVEN WOES ON THE TEACHERS OF THE LAW AND THE PHARISEES

"Woe to you, teachers of the law and Pharisees, you hypocrites! You shut the door of the kingdom of heaven in people's faces. You yourselves do not enter, nor will you let those enter who are trying to.

"Woe to you, teachers of the law and Pharisees, you hypocrites! You travel over land and sea to win a single convert, and when you have succeeded, you make them twice as much a child of hell as you are.

"Woe to you, blind guides! You say, 'If anyone swears by the temple, it means nothing; but anyone who swears by the gold of the temple is bound by that oath.' You blind fools! Which is greater: the gold, or the temple that makes the gold sacred? You also say, 'If anyone swears by the altar, it means nothing; but anyone who swears by the gift on the altar is bound by that oath.' You blind men! Which is greater: the gift, or the altar that makes the gift sacred? Therefore, anyone who swears by the altar swears by it and by everything on it. And anyone who swears by the temple swears by it and by the one who dwells in it. And anyone who swears by heaven swears by God's throne and by the one who sits on it.

"Woe to you, teachers of the law and Pharisees, you hypocrites! You give a tenth of your spices—mint, dill, and cumin. But you have neglected the more important matters of the law—justice, mercy, and faithfulness. You should have practiced the latter, without neglecting the former. You blind guides! You strain out a gnat but swallow a camel.

"Woe to you, teachers of the law and Pharisees, you hypocrites! You clean the outside of the cup and dish, but inside they are full of greed and self-indulgence. Blind Pharisee! First, clean the inside of the cup and dish, and then the outside also will be clean.

"Woe to you, teachers of the law and Pharisees, you hypocrites! You are like whitewashed tombs, which look beautiful on the outside but on the inside are full of the bones of the dead and everything unclean. In the same way, on the outside, you appear to people as righteous, but on the inside, you are full of hypocrisy and wickedness.

"Woe to you, teachers of the law and Pharisees, you hypocrites! You build tombs for the prophets and decorate the graves of the righteous. And you say, 'If we had lived in the days of our ancestors, we would not have taken part with them in shedding the blood of the prophets.' So you testify against yourselves that you are the descendants of those who murdered the prophets. Go ahead, then, and complete what your ancestors started!

"You snakes! You brood of vipers! How will you escape being condemned to hell? Therefore, I am sending you prophets and sages and teachers. Some of them you will kill and crucify; others you will flog in your synagogues and pursue from town to town. And so, upon you will come all the righteous blood that has been shed on earth, from the blood of righteous Abel to the blood of Zechariah son of Berekiah, whom you murdered between the temple and the altar. Truly I tell you, all this will come on this generation.

"Jerusalem, Jerusalem, you who kill the prophets and stone those sent to you, how often I have longed to gather your children together, as a hen gathers her chicks under her wings, and you were not willing. Look, your house is left to you desolate. For I tell you, you will not see me again until you say, 'Blessed is he who comes in the name of the Lord.'" (Matthew 23:13–38)

A couple of examples of immature Christians—not hypocrites, just immature. Remember, we are all a work in progress!

Like newborn babies, crave pure spiritual milk, so that by it you may grow up in your salvation, now that you have tasted that the Lord is good. (1 Peter 2:2–3)

Brothers and sisters, I could not address you as people who live by the Spirit but as people who are still worldly—mere infants in Christ. (1 Corinthians 3:1)

No other book in the history of the world has claimed to be "living and active" in a person's life.

For the word of God is alive and active. Sharper than any double-edged sword, it penetrates even to dividing soul and spirit, joints and marrow; it judges the thoughts and attitudes of the heart. (Hebrews 4:12)

As for God, his way is perfect: The Lord's word is flawless; he shields all who take refuge in him. (Psalm 18:30)

How can a young person stay on the path of purity? By living according to your word. (Psalm 119:9)

Your word is a lamp for my feet, a light on my path. (Psalm 119:105)

The grass withers and the flowers fall, but the word of our God endures forever. (Isaiah 40:8)

I write to you, dear children, because you know the Father. I write to you, fathers, because you know him who is from the beginning. I write to you, young men, because you are strong, and the word of God lives in you, and you have overcome the evil one. (1 John 2:14)

All Scripture is God-breathed and is useful for teaching, rebuking, correcting and training in righteousness, so that the servant of God may be thoroughly equipped for every good work. (2 Timothy 3:16)

No one with all their good works—in and of themselves—is good enough.

> For all have sinned and fall short of the glory of God.
> (Romans 3:23)
>
> Indeed, there is no one on earth who is righteous,
> no one who does what is right and never sins.
> (Ecclesiastes 7:20)
>
> If we claim to be without sin, we deceive ourselves and
> the truth is not in us. (1 John 1:8)

God has a divine plan and purpose for your life in Him; you are always good enough!

> For you created my inmost being;
> you knit me together in my mother's womb.
> I praise you because I am fearfully and wonderfully made;
> your works are wonderful,
> I know that full well. (Psalm 139:13–14)
>
> For we are God's handiwork, created in Christ Jesus
> to do good works, which God prepared in advance for
> us to do. (Ephesians 2:10)
>
> But you, LORD, are a shield around me,
> my glory, the One who lifts my head high. (Psalm 3:3)
>
> Where is another GOD like you, who pardons the sins
> of the survivors among his people? You cannot stay
> angry with your people, for you love to be merciful.
> Once again you will have compassion on us. You will
> tread our sins beneath your feet; you will throw them
> into the depths of the ocean!
> (Micah 7:18–19) (TLB)

CHAPTER 10

BRINGING IT ALL TOGETHER

Most of us think as we run this gauntlet of life that in the end, we somehow need to have been successful, whatever that term means to you—wealthy, happy, intelligent, and so forth. Here are a few online quotes that I find inspirational regarding money and success.

> THERE IS NOTHING MORE BEAUTIFUL THAN
> SOMEONE WHO GOES OUT OF THEIR WAY TO
> MAKE LIFE BEAUTIFUL FOR OTHERS.
> — MANDY HALE

> SEVEN THINGS MONEY CAN'T BUY
>   A HAPPY FAMILY
>   TRUE LOVE
>   PASSION
>   TIME
>   KNOWLEDGE
>   RESPECT
>   INNER PEACE
> — STEVEN AITCHISON

True wealth is not measured in money or status or power. It is measured in the legacy we leave behind for those we love and those we inspire.

— **Cesar Chavez**

Many people define success as being wealthy or famous. They think that someone who is wealthy is more successful than someone who isn't. As a result, making money becomes their priority. They might even sacrifice other things, such as health or family, in their pursuit of wealth. Attaining wealth and fame, however, is the wrong definition of success.

According to the *Google Snippet* web search, the definition of being successful means achieving your desired visions and planned goals. Furthermore, success can be a certain social status that describes a prosperous person that could also have gained fame for its favorable outcome.

The dictionary describes success as "attaining wealth, prosperity, and/or fame." (*Google Snippet*)

These goals of success are not necessarily wrong or bad if managed and attained properly, but as we ponder the idea of how much is enough, or just how famous we should be as we breathe our last, are wealth and fame really what's going to matter the most? I haven't gotten there yet, but I have a hard time thinking so!

I want to think that where we end up for eternity, and the people and relationships we cultivate here on earth are so much more valuable than the wealth we accumulate or the fame we achieve. I believe that the positive investment people make in the lives of others will far outlive them when they are gone. One will be reverently remembered by one's family, friends, and perfect strangers when one has been used by God to make a substantial impact in other people's lives.

I remember a story that a pastor once used as an analogy for a sermon about respect. He said that when he was in high school, he was an absolute stud on the football field. His nickname was "the Grid." And yes, he was all that! He said he was popular on and off the field at school and in his community; everyone respected him being that he was an athletic legend on the football field.

Just a few years after graduating, he returned to his high school football field on a Friday night to watch a game. He had on his old football jersey and was armed and ready for his reunion and recognition because he knew that everyone would remember him and want to show their adoration for "the Grid." To his amazement, only a few people recognized him or even acknowledged who he was, and they didn't make a big deal about it. The vast majority of the people in the stadium couldn't have cared less. He mentioned he was sitting about five or so rows back in the stands from the field, right on the fifty-yard line. At one time, he stood up and turned around with his hands held high, so everyone could get a view of his special "Grid" jersey and remember. A bunch of people sitting behind him started yelling at him to turn around and sit down because they were trying to watch the game. He said that he then put on his jacket, covering his jersey, and casually watched the game. When it was over, he went home like anybody else, having lost his delusion of grandeur.

The point is that my personal relationship with God gives me a constant reminder to look beyond myself and *attempt* to live without selfish ambition or vain conceit and again *attempt* to live the tall order of considering others better than myself.

KING SOLOMON

When Solomon became king, he asked God for wisdom, and he became the wisest man in the world. King Solomon studied, taught, judged, and wrote. Kings and leaders from other countries would travel for many hundreds of miles to learn from King Solomon or to hear him speak due to his profound wisdom. King Solomon had it all: tremendous intellect, power, fame, and wealth. In his Book of Ecclesiastes, King Solomon takes us on a reflective journey through his life, affirming the value of knowledge, work, and pleasure, but only in their proper place.

Near the end of his life, Solomon looked back with an attitude of humility and repentance. He took stock of his life, hoping to spare his readers the bitterness of learning through personal experience that everything apart from God is empty, hollow, and meaningless, an exercise in futility. Here are his closing statements from the Book of Ecclesiastes:

But, my son, be warned: there is no end of opinions ready to be expressed. Studying them can go on forever and become very exhausting! (Ecclesiastes 12:12)

Here is my final conclusion: fear GOD and obey his commandments, for this is the entire duty of man. For GOD will judge us for everything we do, including every hidden thing, good or bad. (Ecclesiastes 12:13–14)

LET'S GET PRACTICAL

So, what's the difference?

Why would one want such a change, and what is the difference in my friendships with another Christian as opposed to a non-Christian? With mutual, deep-rooted spiritual connection, our friendship goes much deeper.

Through the years, I have had numerous Christian men and women approach me because they were getting beat down with life issues, marriage, or other relationships, priorities, work, and personal crises. When we get together, sometime during our conversation (after the formalities), I will ask them, "How is your walk with God?" The usual response is a long, dragged-out, "Well …." As this person thinks what to say next, I am thinking of a literal *Well, as a deep hole dug into the ground to obtain water! And this is going to be a deep subject!*

A short time later, I would mention my "well" thoughts. We would laugh about it for a minute, and that's when the recovery and restoration in our conversation would begin.

During our conversation, I like to emphasize how we can both think about our approach to life's crises like a pointing finger. It is quite natural that we want to point our accusing index finger at something or someone else, blaming them for our adversity. But we must realize that as we do three fingers are pointing back at us, with the most important finger, the thumb, pointing upward toward God. So, we start with our relationship with God. We can then consider those three fingers pointing back at us. And then—and only then—we should take a look at where the index finger is pointing—out in front of us, toward someone else. We both know and understand where our hope and strength will come from as we pick up the broken pieces in our lives and attempt to repair these broken issues and relationships.

I have also had friends come to me and want to talk about the same or similar issues going on in their lives as well, who don't have a relationship with God and don't understand. The difference is that it wouldn't be at all effective to ask them the same question: "How is your walk with God?" That statement would be unconventional for them, and they would not be able to connect at the same level or interval. This is not to say that people who possess a relationship with God are necessarily better or more intelligent than people who don't, yet a person's hope and strength for restoration is entirely different. There is no comparison between the two scenarios when a relationship with God is involved.

Just how effective can anyone be in dealing with life's adversities if they are already tainted, bruised, and beaten down, and are looking for answers only within themselves or with limited exterior resources. As I am all caught up in trying to find a solution to my messed-up turmoil, my focus is on me and my lifelong survival, so quite frankly, I cannot give you what I don't have! Everybody desires strength in their weaknesses and hope in the face of opposition; it's just a matter of where that source derives from and resources available to them to overcome it.

Every alternative path in life will eventually leave us broke, empty, and searching. Only a relationship with God will provide us with the opportunity for complete healing, restoration, and purification of our entire being—not only to the point of our wholeness but also to a *full and overflowing* spirit so that we can be a strength in the lives of others. As you can see, having a relationship with God is not some mystical, magical wave of the wand over the head kind of nonsense. A relationship with God is exceedingly practical in our everyday lives, just as God intended it to be!

Just in case you are wondering, I can tell you exactly who can perfectly navigate their own life without needing this divine intervention in a personal relationship: anybody without issues. That's right, physically, mentally, or spiritually. Pure and blameless, without errors, flaws, or faults—perfect! That list consists of *nobody*, unless you are severely delusional, a legend in your own mind, and out of touch with reality. You can fight it and make a plethora of different excuses, but it won't change the fact that God loves you just the way you are and desires to have a personal relationship with you—no strings attached!

IS RESPECT FOR GOD ENOUGH?

Somehow, in our culture, we have perpetuated the myth that the value of a person depends on how other people perceive them. By this reasoning, anyone could decide if you are worthy or unworthy. And depending on your sociological and psychological conditions and environments, the perceptions other people have of you will vary drastically. This type of illusion has been used to control people and has caused much unnecessary pain and suffering. People can say what they want, but God is the only one who is qualified to establish the value of a person. We all have to determine where our guidance and personal values will come from.

According to the *Google Snippet* web search, the definition of personal values is: Personal values are the things that are important to us, the characteristics and behaviors that motivate us, and guide our decisions.

I presently work with a ministry called Celebrate Recovery at my local church. Celebrate Recovery is an outstanding Christian-based twelve-step recovery program. Recently I spoke with another participant, and he made a statement I won't soon forget: "Don't stay in your mind; it's a bad neighborhood."

I have heard a bunch of comments from people alluding to their utmost respect for God, including the following:

- I'm putting God in the driver's seat.
- He's the man upstairs.
- I pray to God every night.

Respect is not a trust we give easily and consistently; we do not respect someone unless we see that they are strong, pure, and faithful. God has these qualities and more. He is the essence of every good quality, demonstrating them throughout the history of humanity and lovingly revealing them to us personally.

But God is not just contending for our respect or affirmation as if He needs something from us. We as human beings need respect because it will change who we are and help us contend with life, but it won't change who God is. God is the same—yesterday, today, and forever—and that will never change! We want to give God His due respect *because it makes us feel better.* That way, we can go on doing things and conducting our business our way and not feel quite so guilty about it.

God has never passed on the message of "Just respect Me, and that's enough." That's a message that we fabricated to absolve our lack of surrender or commitment! The more you realize how much God loves you, the easier submission and surrender become. Christ, with His arms outstretched on the cross, was saying, "I love you this much, and I would rather die than live without you." Surrendering to Him brings immense freedom, not bondage!

God does not ask only for our respect; what He does require is our total submission and surrender. Any half-hearted commitment will only leave us in the same condition, empty and still searching, with a lot of needless baggage and burdens to have to carry around for the rest of our lives.

The Gospel message, or "Good News," can be summed up in one

sentence: "Jesus died for our sins and rose from the dead." If it sounds extreme, that's because it *is* extreme! *Jesus paid a debt He didn't owe because we owed a debt that we couldn't pay.* Only God Himself could pay that sin debt in full and completely free us from the bondage of sin and shame, and God went there, to the extreme, because He loves you and me that much.

YOU ARE ON HIS MIND

Every human being, regardless of race, creed, gender, or anything else, has equal access to a life-changing relationship with God. That fact, in and of itself is phenomenal. Nothing and nobody else has the capability of fulfilling your most prominent need to be truly loved and fully accepted. That fulfillment will only be permanent and lasting if it generates from the inside.

At this point, go ahead and pinch yourself—not hard, no need to draw blood—on your hand, arm, leg, or wherever. You are a human being, flesh and blood, and that qualifies you for the greatest gift ever offered to humanity: salvation! You qualify not because you are good, smart, or for any other reason apart from God's love for humanity and His abundant grace and mercy. *Grace* is love that seeks you out when you have nothing to give in return, loving you when you are unlovable. *Mercy* is total deliverance from judgment.

Throughout our time together, we have taken a challenging but educational and eye-opening journey. We have traveled through the worst neighborhoods and back alleys of our hearts and minds. We have taken an in-depth and serious look at who we are and who God is. Respect for our fellow human beings is important, but we need so much more than just respect. My hope and prayer are that as you have taken this journey, you have realized that you do not need to look any further to find every human being's ultimate fulfillment. Jesus went to the cross not only to save you but also to transform your life. God always has the best in store for you.

TIME TO MAKE A DECISION

Staying on the fence will only get you splinters!

The following information is taken partly from Evan Tell Ministry.

Your value is precious and established by God. Because of our sin, we cannot, in any sense, earn salvation. We are incapable of paying our sin debt to God or cleansing ourselves from sin. That is why Jesus had to die in our place as our substitute. God requires one step of us—receiving Jesus Christ as our Savior from sin and fully trusting in Him alone as the way of salvation. The Gospel message is simple and so straightforward that a child could easily understand it. The Gospel, or "Good News," can be summed up in one sentence: "Jesus died for our sin and rose from the dead."

Romans 3:23 says, "For all have sinned and fall short of the glory of God."

The word *sin* in the Bible means "miss the mark." God has a standard of absolute perfection in this divine relationship that no human being can meet. We have all sinned and fallen short of God's perfect glory!

Romans 6:23 says, "For the wages of sin is death, but the gift of God is eternal life in Christ Jesus our Lord."

The Bible is saying that because you and I have sinned, we are going to die and be eternally separated from God.

This is bad news, but God never wanted you to be separated from Him. Since there was no way that we could come to God, God decided to come to us.

Romans 5:8 says, "But God demonstrates his own love for us in this: While we were still sinners, Christ died for us."

The Bible is saying that Christ came into the world and took the penalty for sin that was causing our death. He placed it upon Himself, and He died in our place. He was our substitute! He died for us not when we cleaned up our act or did better—*while we were still sinners, just the way we are right now!*

> **Romans 10:9–10** says, "If you declare with your mouth, 'Jesus is Lord,' and believe in your heart that God raised Him from the dead, you will be saved. For it is with your heart that you believe and are justified, and it is with your mouth that you profess your faith and are saved."

What is faith? The word *faith* means trust. *Saved* means to be rescued or delivered from the penalty of sin. Putting your faith in Christ means trusting Him to save you. Once we enter into this holy and divine relationship, our eternal destiny is to be in God's presence.

I hope and pray that you don't miss out on the greatest gift ever offered humanity!

Please bear in mind that if you have now trusted Jesus, you are saved. You have transferred your trust from whatever it was in, to the person of Christ, and God has declared you justified, redeemed, and saved.

Praying now is a great way to solidify your decision to trust Christ. Don't keep it a secret—tell somebody. If someone else has been praying or spoken to you about a life-changing relationship with God, tell them about your decision to trust Christ—they will be ecstatic!

EXAMPLE: PRAYER OF SALVATION

> *Dear God, I know that I am a sinner. Nothing I am or do makes me deserve heaven or this life-changing relationship with you. I believe Jesus died for me and rose from the dead, and right now, I trust Jesus Christ alone as my Savior and Lord of my life forever. Thank You for this forgiveness and everlasting life that I now possess. In Jesus's name, amen.*

Now go ahead and find a *healthy* non-denominational church (not perfect; they don't exist!) that teaches the Bible and get involved. You need them, and they need you!

I have a message for those of you who have already trusted Christ but have been distant or walked away from God for any reason. I hope you know that He has been waiting for you with open arms; He's been there the whole time! He won't walk away, but you have. You know that your life hasn't been right, and there is a big gaping void. I sure hope you have left all your irrational thinking and neglect back in your Samaria and walked away from it. So, come on back home where your fulfillment awaits and where you belong.

EXAMPLE: PRAYER OF REDEDICATION

> *Dear God, I have been distant from You. I know that You will never leave me or turn Your back on me. I miss our time of intimate fellowship. God, please restore in me a pure heart and renew a right spirit within me. Thank You for Your divine restoration and healing power. In Jesus's name, amen.*

For those who choose to remain skeptics, I would like to offer you a challenge. For the next sixty days or longer, read a chapter in the New Testament Book of John. John is twenty-one chapters, so you should make it through the entire book about three times. During your reading, put God to the test. Ask Jesus to reveal Himself to you. Jesus endured rejection, flogging, and crucifixion, just to name part of the humiliation that He suffered. So, I am sure He is not excessively concerned about you putting Him to the test.

Whether you are just starting with God on this new life-changing journey, have rededicated your life and returned to where you belong, or are still seeking, may our great God and Savior truly bless and honor you and yours. May you soar on wings like eagles, run and not grow weary, and walk and not be faint as you seek, submit, and abide in Him.

ARTHUR H. MOONEYHAN

In him, we have redemption through his blood, the forgiveness of sins, in accordance with the riches of God's grace. (Ephesians 1:7)

In him and through faith in him we may approach God with freedom and confidence. (Ephesians 3:12)

Don't be selfish; don't live to make a good impression on others. Be humble, thinking of others as better than yourself. (Philippians 2:3) (TLB)

Now to him who is able to do immeasurably more than all we ask or imagine, according to his power that is at work within us, to him be glory in the church and in Christ Jesus throughout all generations, forever and ever! Amen. (Ephesians 3: 20–21)

But the man who isn't a Christian can't understand and can't accept these thoughts from God, which the Holy Spirit teaches us. They sound foolish to him because only those who have the Holy Spirit within them can understand what the Holy Spirit means. Others just can't take it in.
(1 Corinthians 2:14) (TLB)

Let him have all your worries and cares, for he is always thinking about you and watching everything that concerns you. 1 Peter 5:7). (TLB)

Come to me, all you who are weary and burdened, and I will give you rest. Take my yoke upon you and learn from me, for I am gentle and humble in heart, and you will find rest for your souls. (Matthew 11:28–29)

For great is your love, higher than the heavens;
your faithfulness reaches to the skies. (Psalm 108:4)

Trust in the LORD with all your heart
and lean not on your own understanding;
in all your ways submit to him,
and he will make your paths straight. (Proverbs 3:5–6)

Show me your ways, LORD,
teach me your paths.
Guide me in your truth and teach me,
for you are GOD my Savior,
and my hope is in you all day long. (Psalm 25:4–5)

My flesh and my heart may fail,
but GOD is the strength of my heart
and my portion forever. (Psalm 73:26)

But those who hope in the LORD
will renew their strength.
They will soar on wings like eagles;
they will run and not grow weary,
they will walk and not be faint. (Isaiah 40:31)

And how does a man benefit if he gains the whole
world and loses his soul in the process? For is anything
worth more than his soul? (Mark 8:36–37) (TLB)